# INSIGHT COMPACT GUIDE

CW00336727

& THE

*Compact Guide: Cancún & the Yucatán* is the ultimate quick-reference guide to this part of Mexico. It tells you everything you need to know about the city and its region, from modern resorts to ancient Maya ruins, coral reefs to underground caverns, colonial cities to dense jungle, and great beaches to pulsating nightlife.

This is one of 130 Compact Guides, combining the interests and enthusiasms of two of the world's best-known information providers: Insight Guides, whose innovative titles have set the standard for visual travel guides since 1970, and Discovery Channel, the world's premier source of nonfiction television programming.

Discovery
CHANNEL

APA PUBLICATIONS
Part of the Langenscheidt Publishing Group

# Insight Compact Guide: Cancún

*Written by:* Tony Halliday with Bronwen Hillman
*Photography by:* Glyn Genin
*Additional photography by:* Tony Halliday; also Marcus Wilson-Smith/
Apa *(8, 31/2, 60/1, 63/2, 64/2, 67, 71)*; Luis Gomez Cardenas
*(13/2, 31/1, 45)*; Pete Bennett *(54)*; Dave Houser *(104)*; courtesy of
Hidden Worlds Cenotes *(9)*; courtesy of Xcaret *(10, 13/1, 14/1, 36)*;
courtesy of Coco Bongo *(25)*
*Cover picture by:* Chuck Place
*Maps:* Stephen Ramsay
*Cartographic Editor:* Maria Randell
*Design concept:* Carlotta Junger
*Picture Editor:* Hilary Genin

*Editorial Director:* Brian Bell

**CONTACTING THE EDITORS:** As every effort is made to provide accurate
information in this publication, we would appreciate it if readers would
call our attention to any errors and omissions by contacting:
*Apa Publications, PO Box 7910, London SE1 1WE, England.*
*Fax: (44 20) 7403 0290; e-mail: insight@apaguide.demon.co.uk*

Information has been obtained from sources believed to be reliable,
but its accuracy and completeness, and the opinions based thereon,
are not guaranteed.

© 2002 APA Publications GmbH & Co. Verlag KG Singapore Branch, Singapore.
*First Edition 2002*
*Printed in Singapore by:* Insight Print Services (Pte) Ltd

Distributed in the United States by:
**Langenscheidt Publishers, Inc.**
46–35 54th Road, Maspeth, NY 11378
Tel: (1-718) 784 0055, fax: (1-718) 784 0640

Distributed in the UK & Ireland by:
**GeoCenter International Ltd**
The Viables Centre, Harrow Way, Basingstoke,
Hampshire RG22 4BJ
Tel: (44-1256) 817 987, fax: (44-1256) 817 988

Worldwide distribution enquiries:
**APA Publications GmbH & Co. Verlag KG (Singapore Branch)**
38 Joo Koon Road, Singapore 628990
Tel: (65) 6865 1600, fax: (65) 6861 6438

# www.insightguides.com

# Cancún
## & The Yucatán

△ **Cancún (p22)** White beaches and turquoise waters are the hallmark not just of Cancún, but of the entire Riviera Maya.

▷ **Mesoamerican Reef (p12)** The second-longest reef system in the world stretches all along the Caribbean coast.

▽ **Mérida (p68)** Capital of Yucatán province, a city full of colonial treasures and bursting with vitality.

▷ **Chichén Itzá (p60)** One of the world's great archeological sites is just a few hours from Cancún. The picture shows the Pyramid of Kukulcán, a giant timepiece oriented to the heavens.

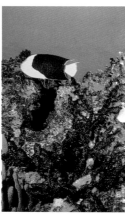

▷ **Izamal (p56)** With its colonial architecture alongside the ruins of ancient pyramids, this is where two worlds meet.

△ **Hidden Worlds (p41)** An amazing complex of underwater caverns that can be explored by both divers and snorkelers.

▷ **Uxmal (p84)** The largest Classic Maya site in the Yucatán, renowned for its colossal architecture and decorative detail.

△ **Celestún (p75)** With its mangroves and lagoons, flamingos and other birds, this is a great place for a tour on the wild side.

▷ **Tulum (p41)** Famous for its dramatic Maya ruins, Tulum also has miles of sandy beaches.

▽ **Xcaret (p37)** This nature park, with its huge variety of activities and attractions, also brings to life the world of the ancient Maya.

# Beach and Other Cultures

The most vivid impression gained by visitors to Cancún is the feel of its sand and the color of its water. Walking on the beach here is like treading through the finest talcum powder, and no matter how hot the sun gets, the sand has the unique characteristic of staying cool. No need for any protective footwear; just let it all trickle between your toes. The water is equally enticing: when the sun shines, as it usually does on about 300 days a year, it takes on a vibrant turquoise color with an incredible translucence. And this being the tropics, it's always warm. Welcome to Cancún.

Until the late 1960s, this narrow island, located at the northeastern tip of Mexico's Yucatán Peninsula, was a remote backwater inhabited only by small enclaves of Maya who tapped the trees for gum sap, and loggers who extracted the local hardwood. It is now an international tourism playground, with some of the world's most extravagant luxury hotels and activities to suit every taste.

But for visitors to this part of Mexico there is much more to explore than just Cancún. The eastern coast of the peninsula, with its variety of settlements and resorts, has the same – or even better – paradise beaches. It has been dubbed the Riviera Maya, a hint to the fact that the attractions of the region are not limited to the beach. Both Cancún and the Riviera are gateways to the rich legacy of the fascinating Maya civilization. The Spanish colonial heritage is also evident in towns across the peninsula. Ancient pyramids, stately mansions, haciendas and convents can be as much a part of a visit to Cancún as sun, sea and sand.

## LOCATION AND SIZE

The Yucatán Peninsula begins in the southeastern part of Mexico, reaching out into the Gulf of Mexico and the Caribbean Sea. The peninsula is bordered by Belize and Guatemala in the south, and covers an area of 146,498 sq km (56,563 sq miles). It is

**What's in a name?**
The name Yucatán was given to the peninsula by the first Spanish explorers. Assuming everyone could speak Spanish, the ship's captain asked the local Maya 'What is the name of this place?' 'Ci-u-than' was the reply, meaning, 'we don't understand you'. The Spanish assumed this was the answer.

*Opposite: Cancún's color*
*Below: typical fishing boat*

occupied by three Mexican states: Quintana Roo (50,350 sq km/19, 440 sq miles), Yucatán (39,340 sq km/15,189 sq miles) and Campeche (56,798 sq km/21,930 sq miles). Chetumal, Mérida and Campeche are the respective state capitals. Cancún and the Riviera Maya are located within Quintana Roo. A number of islands lie off the coast, the most notable ones being Cozumel and Isla Mujeres. Though technically an island, Cancún itself is connected to the mainland by causeways.

*Relaxation in a hammock*

## CLIMATE

The Yucatán is warm and sunny all year round, though there are temperature and precipitation variations that broadly divide the year into two seasons. Conditions are generally drier and cooler from November to April, when the average high temperatures are in the mid-80s°F (29°C) with lows in the upper 60s°F (19°–20°C). It gets hotter and more humid, with a greater chance of rain, between May and October, with highs of around 90°F (32°C) and lows in the mid-70s°F (24°C). If it comes at all, the rain usually falls in the afternoon or at night in short, sharp bursts. September and October are the rainiest months as well as the most likely months for hurricanes and storms. However, the odds of a hurricane striking a particular destination on any given date are low.

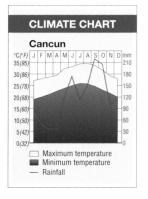

### CLIMATE CHART

**Cancun**

°C(°F) J F M A M J J A S O N D mm
35(95) 210
30(86) 180
25(78) 150
20(68) 120
15(60) 90
10(50) 60
5(42) 30
0(32) 0

☐ Maximum temperature
■ Minimum temperature
— Rainfall

## WHEN TO GO

The tourism calendar reflects the climatic differences outlined, with high season coinciding with the winter months, low season with summer and fall. During the high season, hotel rates at the main tourist centers can double or even treble, which may be a consideration. However, being cooler the high season is definitely easier for traveling, particularly if you're exploring inland towns and villages or hacking through jungle to archeological sites. Low season rates are enticing, but you do have a greater chance of rain. The hottest and stickiest month is May, but this is also the time when tropical fruits are at their best.

# GEOLOGY

The Yucatán is predominantly flat. Formed of limestone laid down in ancient sea beds, much of the northern part of the peninsula hardly rises more than a few meters above sea level. There is a small range of hills, the Puuc Hills, in the central-western part of the peninsula, but apart from these and the gradually higher elevations towards the south, the only landmarks of any size are the pyramids left behind by the ancient Maya.

## CAVES AND CENOTES

As far as geology is concerned, the really interesting features of the landscape lie beneath the surface. Acting like a giant sponge, with no surface drainage except along the southern border, the Yucatán is riddled with cave systems and sinkholes. Some of the caverns are dramatic with superb stalactite and stalagmite formations. The sinkholes are the result of the roof of an underground cavern collapsing. Known locally as cenotes (corrupted from the Maya word *dzonot* by the Spanish), these are and always have been a major source of water for the local inhabitants; indeed the traditional settlement pattern was based on the existence of cenotes. In ancient times, the waters from the sinkholes were held to be sacred; at some cenotes within archeological sites, vestiges

**Deep impact**

Some 65 million years ago, a huge meteor plunged to earth just off the present coast of northern Yucatán, forming a crater over 250km (155 miles) in diameter. Some scientists believe that the huge amounts of dust thrown up by the impact brought about the extinction of the dinosaurs, but whatever the merits of that theory, the effect on the structure of the Yucatán was profound. The flat northern part of the peninsula is part of the crater base; the rim of the crater, visible in the shape of the Puuc Hills, created a north-south divide which today causes the subterranean rivers of the peninsula to deposit their water either in the Gulf of Mexico or the Caribbean Sea. There is a related theory that the cenotes are not collapsed caverns at all but potholes created by large chunks of debris falling from the meteor as it descended to earth.

*Cavern diving at Hidden Worlds near Tulum*

*Below: a scarlet macaw*
*Bottom: the jaguar was held*
*to be sacred by the*
*ancient Maya*

of ancient pottery and human remains indicat that they may have been used for religious sac rifical rites. Today locals and visitors alike us them as swimming pools, or even for diving an snorkeling. The Hidden Worlds Cenotes nea Tulum, for example, a combined complex o underwater caves and cenotes, offers some o the best cave diving in the world.

The geology of the Yucatán also explains wh the waters surrounding the peninsula are so crys tal clear, particularly on the Caribbean side. Th fact that there is no surface run-off means tha there is no silt carried into the sea.

## FLORA AND FAUNA

The surface of the flat northern limestone sla of the peninsula is capped by a tangle of low jun gle, or *monte* as the locals call it. Further south in the Puuc Hills and beyond, the jungle become denser, and the trees, including various tropica hardwood species, higher. The *chicozapote* tree which the Maya cultivated for use in building a well for the extraction of chicle, the natural chew ing gum resin, grows all over the Yucatán. Unt the introduction of synthetic resin, this was a goo source of income locally.

The jungle environment provides the habita for an astonishing array of flora and fauna. Plar

life includes the bright orange *ciricote*, the state plant of Quintana Roo, found throughout the low and medium forests of the peninsula alongside numerous vareties of orchid. The color of the vegetation is matched by that of the birds, including the toucan which is common in the northern part of the peninsula; distinctive for its long curved beak and brilliant color, it emits sounds resembling a frog's croak rather than birdsong. Parrots and macaws are common in the denser jungle areas, where they are joined in the trees by spider monkeys and howler monkeys. Stalking the undergrowth are various feline species, including the jaguar. The jaguar was held to be sacred by the ancient Maya; its pelt was even donned as a disguise by shamans in religious ceremonies.

In the far south of the Yucatán, both flora and fauna are protected in the Calakmul Biosphere Reserve. With an area of 800,000 hectares (2 million acres), this is the second largest protected area in Mexico, and is contiguous with 1.3 million more hectares (3.2 million acres) of forest reserves in Guatemala and Belize. While all wildlife here is protected, efforts are focused on preserving the local jaguar population. Being home to the largest concentration of Maya ruins anywhere in Mesoamerica, the reserve has been opened up to tourism, and when exploring the great Maya ruins of Calakmul, for example *(see page 98)*, you have the opportunity of seeing, or at least hearing, jungle life at close quarters.

## COASTAL RESERVES

Despite the pressures of tourism, much of the Yucatán's coastline is still in a pristine state. As well as miles and miles of sandy beaches, there are long stretches of coast that are preserved as natural parks or as biosphere reserves. The main ones in the north are **Río Lagartos** and **Celestún**, where protected lagoons and mangroves provide a haven for a rich variety of bird and animal life. The fragile ecosystem of the lagoons, with their shallow hypersaline waters, provides the perfect habitat for the pink flamingo, flocks of which can

**Mangroves**
The lagoon and estuary mangroves of the Yucatán belong to one of the most productive ecosystems on earth. Mangroves are highly efficient converters of sunlight into organic material. This material in turn feeds countless invertebrates, which are themselves consumed by numerous fish, bird and mammal species. Mangroves are resistant to salt water, and thus prosper where other plants cannot. They are also adapted to anaerobic (oxygen poor) soil conditions. The black mangrove *(Avicennia germinans)* sends up straw-like shoots that bring oxygen to its roots; the red mangrove *(Rhizophora mangle)* has similar 'breathing holes' in its arching, aerial roots.

*A great egret perches in the mangroves of Río Lagartos*

**Salt waters**

The lagoons are used as shelters by fishermen for their boats, just as the ancient Maya used them, when they plied the coastal waters in dugout canoes, trading goods from the shores of the Gulf of Mexico all the way to Central America. The major export in ancient times was salt, much of which was produced in the extensive flats behind Las Coloradas within today's Rio Lagartos Biosphere Reserve. Las Coloradas is now the second-largest producer of salt in Mexico.

*The ubiquitous iguana*

be spotted in these areas all year round. Other common birds include kingfishers, cormorants, frigate birds, herons, egrets, white ibises, ospreys, hawks and pelicans. The lagoons also serve as natural nurseries for an abundance of fish, crab and mollusc species, and though its numbers have dwindled, the American crocodile is also found in these waters.

In the southeast of the peninsula is the huge expanse of the Sian Ka'an Biosphere Reserve. Sian Ka'an is the Maya for 'Birthplace of the Sky', and with an area of 520,000 hectares (1.3 million acres), this is the third-largest protected area in Mexico. The reserve covers a large chunk of the mainland with its myriad islands, lagoons and mangrove forests, and boasts an impressive variety of plant and animal life with over 1,200 types of flora, 340 species of birds, and 103 different species of animals, including lobster, manatees, jaguars, ocelots, and crocodiles. Like Calakmul, the Sian Ka'an occupies land once inhabited by the ancient Maya. More than 20 Maya sites are to be found here, as well some more 'modern' indigenous villages. Local farmers have learned from their ancestors and are applying ancient farming methods to present-day agriculture.

## THE MESOAMERICAN REEF

The Sian Ka'an also incorporates a 100km- (62-mile-) long section of the Mesoamerican Reef, also called the Great Maya Reef. For many people, this coral reef, the second-longest in the world after Australia's Great Barrier Reef, is the Yucatán's greatest natural treasure. Extending for more than 1,000km (620 miles) from Isla Mujeres in the north to Honduran waters in the south, the reef is home to a bewildering variety of sea life, all of it vital to the maintenance of a highly fragile ecosystem, where even a small variation in the water temperature can cause a life-threatening drama.

Larger denizens of this fabulous underwater forest include various kinds of shark (bull, nurse, reef and hammerhead); various species of stingrays; moray eels, which lurk in crevices; and predatory barracudas which feed off schools of small fish. The latter come in all colors of the rainbow: the blue angel fish, the reef butterfly; the doctorfish; the inflatable porcupine fish; the striped sergeant major, the atlantic spadefish; the bridled goby; the hogfish; the honeycomb cowfish and the magnificent rainbow parrotfish are just some of the exotic species that make the Mesoamerican Reef such a paradise for divers and snorkelers. Excursions to the reef can be made from Cancún, Isla Mujeres, Puerto Morelos, Playa del Carmen, Cozumel and many other centers along the Riviera.

## TURTLE BEACHES

Lying as it does just off the coast (you can see the waves breaking over it from many beaches along the Riviera), the Mesoamerican Reef forms a natural barrier, calming the Caribbean waves and protecting the beaches from erosion. It is this protected environment that has helped spawn the beach resorts, but it has also been responsible for attracting turtles to lay their eggs in the soft, white sands. Of the eight species of turtle surviving in the world, four nest on the coasts of the Yucatán: the green turtle, loggerhead turtle, hawksbill turtle and leatherback turtle. Turtles spend their whole life in the water except for the

*Below: a hawksbill turtle*
*Bottom: common reef fish include the striped sergeant major*

brief moments when females come ashore to nest and lay their eggs. They arrive at various points along the north coast as well as the Riviera. One of their favorite spots is Akumal, where tourism development has created a clear conflict between human and turtle needs. Nevertheless, strenuous efforts are being made to ensure that the turtles keep coming back.

*Below: swimming in the Maya River at Xcaret*
*Bottom: walkway at Xel-Há*

## INLETS AND ECOPARKS

Apart from the beaches, lagoons and reef, the most notable feature of the Yucatán are the brackish inlets that punctuate the coast of the Riviera. Fed by the underground river systems of the interior, their mix of fresh and saltwater creates a fascinating marine environment. The most spectacular inlet is Xel-Há ('the place where water is born') north of Tulum. Once used as a port by the Maya, it has now been developed, albeit very sensitively, into a major tourist attraction, where visitors can swim with the fish in what's billed as the 'largest natural aquarium in the world'. Also occupying an inlet, and complete with its own undergound river, is Xcaret near Playa del Carmen. With its multitude of activities and spectacular evening shows of folkloric dancing and Maya rituals, this is one of the top attractions of the Riviera Maya.

## LOST PYRAMIDS

There are few places in the world where the past feels as close as it does in the Yucatán. Even in the Hotel Zone of Cancún, among the concrete and glass constructions of the post-modern era, there is an ancient Maya ruin. The beach palapas where you drink your cocktails are built according to Maya principles of design, and the little thatched houses that you pass along country roads when venturing into the interior are practically the same as the ones ordinary people would have lived in 3,000 years ago.

The Maya have left their legacy all over the Yucatán. Their civilization, which began in the region around 1500BC and encompassed present-day southern Mexico, Guatemala, northern Belize and western Honduras, is the best known of the classical civilizations of Mesoamerica. Noted for their elaborate ceremonial architecture, including temple-pyramids, palaces and observatories, the Maya built on the inherited inventions and ideas of earlier civilizations such as the Olmec. The developments they made in astronomy, in organizing their calendar, in mathematics and in hieroglyphic writing were unique in the ancient world.

However, by the time of the arrival of the Spanish in the early 16th century, internal conflict had already resulted in the decline of High Maya civilization. Great cities like Chichén Itzá and Uxmal were forgotten and left to decay in the jungle, only again seeing the light of day when explorers stumbled across them in the early 19th century *(see panel on right)*. The explorers gave way to archeologists, and the archeologists of today are still uncovering ruins in the Yucatán jungle.

## THE SPANISH LEGACY

The other great attraction of the Yucatán are its Spanish colonial towns and cities, like Mérida, Valladolid, Izamal and Campeche. The Yucatán was the Spaniards' first landfall on the mainland of the New World. Juan de Grijalva, a sea captain, landed on Cozumel in 1518 and proceeded to sail round the peninsula, hearing tales of the New

### Explorers

Having been lost to the jungle, the Maya ruins lay undisturbed for nearly one thousand years until their rediscovery by intrepid explorers in the early 19th century. Though he was not the first to visit the Maya sites, it was the Bostonian traveler John Stephens who first introduced them to a wider public through his writings, most notably *Incidents of Travel in Central America, Chiapas and Yucatán* (1841). Stephens was accompanied on his expeditions by British architect Frederick Catherwood, who produced beautifully detailed lithographs of the sites they surveyed. Their tales of discovery of lost cities in the jungle encouraged other pioneers to the region, including the French photographer Desiré Charnay, who hacked through the jungles with early camera equipment.

*A lithograph by Catherwood of the Xtacumbilxunán caves*

### The Talking Cross

After the War of the Castes, the Maya continued to resist white domination for more than a generation, taking refuge in the jungles of Quintana Roo. Here a sect developed, the Chan Santa Cruz group, based on ancient Maya beliefs and Christian teachings. At its heart was the Talking Cross, from which sacred wood great words of wisdom would spout. The holy voice was actually a ventriloquist who inspired the Maya to continue their fight and issued strategic orders. It was not until 1934 that the last rebels signed a peace treaty – shortly before Quintana Roo became a territory.

*Church facade on the Convent Route*

World's untold riches. The conquistador Hernán Cortés followed a year later, but it was left to Don Francisco de Montejo, a gentleman of Seville, to take possession of the Yucatán in the name of the Spanish king, in 1527. Starting with Mérida in 1542, the Spanish laid out their towns around convents and churches constructed from the rubble of ancient pyramids. While imposing Christianity on the natives, they denounced Maya rituals as heathen, and destroyed their idols and scriptures. But the biggest blow to the Maya came with diseases the Spaniards brought with them, previously unknown in the New World. Smallpox, influenza and measles rapidly decimated the local population, soon reduced to working as slaves on tobacco and sugarcane plantations.

Centuries of exploitation followed. The Maya gradually lost their lands and their elders were stripped of their positions. In 1848 they revolted, and the bloody War of the Castes resulted in the whites temporarily losing control of all of the Yucatán except Mérida and Campeche.

## THE HENEQUEN ERA

With the coming of Independence, the Yucatán lost its traditional trade markets – Spain, Cuba and Mexico City – so new sources of income had to be found. Prosperity arrived in the shape of the henequen plant, which had been used by the Maya for centuries for making rope, but whose commercial potential for shipping and international trade was now realized.

Yucatán was the main producer, exporting the rope fibres through the north coast port of Sisal, after which processed henequen soon became known around the world. The 'green gold' made Mérida one of the richest cities per capita in the world; it also reinforced the status of the Maya as mere slaves, forced to work on the hacienda plantations for a pittance. Today most of the henequen haciendas lie abandoned and crumbling, though some have been converted into hotels. The villages that grew up around them are still there, populated by descendants of the plantation workers.

## YUCATAN TODAY

Their cities may have crumbled, but the descendants of the temple builders, astronomers, mathematicians, artisans and farmers still inhabit the Yucatán today, alongside the majority *mestizo* population (people of mixed Maya and European descent) and a small minority of people of pure European ancestry. Many Maya continue to speak the old language, and their faith is expressed through a modern Christian-Maya hybrid. Local village traditions include the old shamanic rituals, still employed for healing or during times of drought. Visitors will come face to face with Maya culture in local handicrafts, in elements of clothing, as well as in the local cuisine.

While most Maya still live in relative poverty, struggling for their rights, it is paradoxically a new invasion, tourism, that has contributed to a new-found confidence. Centered on Cancún and the Riviera Maya, tourism is now the main industry of the Yucatán, and there is no doubt that the presence of the Maya as a living culture has engendered new respect and understanding, not just for the people themselves, but for their past, their traditions and their environment. In a region whose history has been marked by conflict, the Maya legacy still has a role to play, particularly in the latest battle – that between the demands of development and conservation.

*Below: children in Tecoh
Bottom: the Ball Court
at the Maya city of Cobá*

# HISTORICAL HIGHLIGHTS

**From 5,200BC** Nomadic hunters of Asiatic origin settle in what is now modern Mexico, domesticating cattle and cultivating corn, beans, chili peppers and squash.

**2,000BC** The rise of the Olmec civilization, from which many aspects of Maya culture are derived, including the development of village farming, the construction of pyramid temples and the creation of a calendar based on a 52-year cycle.

**1,500BC** The group that comes to be known as the Maya settles in an area stretching from the Pacific coast to the southern Yucatán, taking in modern-day Guatemala, Belize, Honduras and the Mexican states of Chiapas and Campeche. In the ensuing centuries they migrate into the northern Yucatán. During the so-called Pre-Classic period (to about 300BC) the Maya develop a complex, hierarchical society, ruled by kings and nobles. The first great cities are built.

## AD300–900
The Classic period of Maya civilization, during which its finest structures are erected across the region, including those at Uxmal, Calakmul, Cobá and Chichén Itzá (Old Chichén). For reasons not fully understood, the civilization declines and many of its cities are abandoned.

## AD900–1200
The northern Yucatán becomes the center of Maya civilization, with Toltec-influenced Chichén Itzá becoming a major regional player.

**1250** The fall of Chichén Itzá and emergence of Mayapán as the principal Maya city of the Yucatán.

**1441** Mayapán is sacked by invaders from Uxmal, precipitating the final decline of the civilization.

**1512** A shipwreck near present-day Chetumal leaves the first two Spaniards, Gonzalo Guerrero and Jerónimo de Aguilar, among the Maya of the Yucatán. The family Guerrero forms with his Maya wife is the beginning of the mixed race or *mestizaje* of Mexico.

**1517** Arrival on the coast of Yucatán of Francisco Hernandez de Córdoba, who encounters fierce resistance from the local Maya at Campeche.

**1519** Hernán Cortés arrives on the island of Cozumel, off the Yucatán coast, at the start of the discovery and conquest of Mexico.

**1527** Don Francisco de Montejo, a gentleman of Seville, takes possession of the Yucatán in the name of the Spanish king.

**1540** Campeche founded by Francisco de Montejo the Younger, on the site of a Maya trading village. The town becomes the peninsula's gateway for shipping.

**1542** Foundation of Mérida by Francisco de Montejo the Younger over the ancient Maya city of Th'o. Mérida becomes the Spanish capital of the Yucatán.

**1540s** Franciscan Friars set out to bring Christianity to the Maya, starting with the Xíu Maya who inhabit villages to the south of Mérida. Bishop Diego de Landa publishes *Relación de las cosas de Yucatán*, an invaluable insight into the Maya way of life. But from his base in Izamal, de Landa also subjects the Maya to cruel persecution.

**1562** Organized by Bishop de Landa, the burning of Maya manuscripts and icons outside the church of San Miguel Arcángel in Maní destroys virtually all Maya recorded history in a single night.

**1739** First of the surviving Maya manuscripts rediscovered in Vienna and taken to the German city of Dresden, to become known as the Dresden codex.

**1821** Mexico wins independence from Spain. Two years later, having initially desired to join a Central American Federation, Yucatán becomes a state of the new nation.

**1841** The publication of *Incidents of Travel in Central America Chiapas and Yucatán* by explorer John Stephens, illustrated by Frederick Catherwood, begins the era of scientific investigation of the great Maya sites.

**1846** After years of political chaos, Yucatán opts to become independent of the fledgling Mexican state.

**1847** Local landowners arm their Maya peasants to help fight off any Mexican invasion force, but the Maya turn their weapons on their oppressors and the War of the Castes erupts in Valladolid; it spreads quickly throughout the Yucatán until the rebels occupy every town but Mérida and Campeche. Reprisals are brutal and close to a third of the population is wiped out; under the guidance of the 'Talking Cross' cult, armed resistance continues in isolated pockets of the Yucatán until well into the 20th century.

**1863** Campeche becomes a state.

**1880s** Large-scale production of henequen begins on estates around Mérida. While henequen and other cash crops make millionaires out of hacienda owners, the new economic boom only reinforces the subservient role of the Maya, and many ancient cultural traditions and agricultural methods are lost.

**1910** Rampant government corruption leads to the Mexican Revolution.

**1915** The Mexican government extracts millions of pesos from Yucatecan landlords against Pancho Villa and Emiliano Zapata.

**1920–23** Yucatán is governed by revolutionary socialists under the leadership of Felipe Carillo Puerto. His attempts to improve the lives of the Maya majority abruptly end with his assassination by local landowners in 1924.

**1923** First reconstruction work undertaken in Chichén Itzá.

**1937** Mexican president Lázaro Cárdenas orders massive land redistribution in Yucatán.

**1974** Quintana Roo made a Mexican state. First hotels opened in the resort of Cancún, Quintana Roo.

**1993** Izamal near Mérida is chosen by Pope John Paul II as the site of his meeting with the natives of Mexico and Central America during his August visit to the Yucatán. The Pope apologizes for the past suffering of native peoples caused by the policies and actions of the Catholic Church.

**1994** On January 1, Mexico joins the North American Free Trade Agreement with the US and Canada, hailed as Mexico's entrance to the 'first world'. The year also sees the uprising of the Zapatistas in the State of Chiapas.

**2000** Vincente Fox, leader of the National Action Party (PAN), is elected Mexican president, the first since 1929 not to be a member of the Institutional Revolutionary Party (PRI). He promises Mexicans full democracy after 71 years of often autocratic, single-party rule.

Mérida, capital of the state of Yucatán, celebrates a year as the 'Continental Capital of Culture'.

Map on page 24

*Preceding pages: the Maya ruins of Tulum*
*Below: Cancún city hall detail*
*Bottom: Playa Delfines*

# 1: Cancún and Isla Mujeres

There was nothing much in Cancún until the late 1960s, when the National Tourism Development Fund (Fonatur) came to assess the feasibilty of creating a resort here, on a stretch of coast that, while known for its fine beaches and turquoise sea, had hitherto been largely ignored by the Mexican government. The only population center of any size, Mérida, was at that time five hours away, so it wasn't just hotels but a whole new infrastructure that had to be created. Building work began in 1970, and today Cancún's Hotel Zone has become a resort city on a massive scale, a 22 km (14-mile) strip of high-rise hotels, golf courses, marinas, restaurants, nightclubs and shopping malls. Some of the hotels have spectacular designs: the Melia Cancún and Hilton, for example, seek to mimic the architectural legacy of the Maya with their distinctive pyramid shapes.

## LAYOUT

The Hotel Zone occupies an island, shaped like a 7 and linked to the mainland by two bridges, one at Playa Linda in the north and the other at Nizuc Channel in the south. A single road, the Boulevard Kukulcán, runs the length of the narrow island, linking up in the north with the downtown

area of Cancún; this city of 500,000 is the administrative hub, and also has a number of hotels (generally cheaper than in the Hotel Zone) as well as nightclubs, some excellent restaurants and markets. Separating the Hotel Zone from the mainland is the enormous **Nichupté Lagoon** and its two extensions, Bojórquez and Inglés, which combine fresh water fed by underground springs and salt water that enters from two openings to the sea. Here, mangroves provide hiding places for crocodiles, and birdlife is plentiful, with over 200 catalogued species including herons, egrets, ospreys, screaming parrots, and parakeets.

Apart from its beaches and entertainment, the biggest attraction of Cancún lies just off the coast in the shape of the Cancún/Isla Mujeres National Marine Park, part of the giant Mesoamerican Reef *(see pages 12–13)*. Snorkelers and scuba divers are in their element here.

## HOTEL ZONE

Cancún's extravagant hotels and shopping malls have become sightseeing attractions in their own right. But despite the overwhelming resort influence, history is not totally forgotten. As you travel along Blvd. Kukulcán, you might notice a series of monuments set among neatly tended shrubs. These are fibreglass replicas of statues, reliefs and friezes found at various archeological sites throughout the Maya world. And you can even see the real thing: ★**El Rey ❶** at Km 18 (south of the highway opposite the Hilton and next to the golf course), is a small archeological site (open daily 8am–5pm) that provides a good introduction to Maya architecture, containing as it does a number of features common to most larger sites in the Yucatán.

Also known as the Kinich Ahau Group, the King of the Sun's Face, after a carved stone human head found here, the site is made up of two plazas surrounded by buildings and platforms. The buildings seen today date from the late postclassic period (AD1250–1521), and include a palace, whose roofing was held up by 18 columns,

### Beaches

Cancún has seven main beaches. The most sheltered are Playas Langosta, Tortugas and Caracol on Bahía de Mujeres in the north, which are ideal for every type of water sport, and swimmers of all levels of proficiency. On the long eastern side, facing out into the Caribbean between Punta Cancún and Punta Nizuc, are Playas Chac-Mool, Marlin, Ballenas and Delfines. In windy conditions, the waves here are usually larger and the undertow stronger; a yellow flag indicates that caution is needed, while black or red signal that it is dangerous to venture into the sea. Since all beaches are public, a fun excursion is to walk the hotel row, stopping here and there for refreshments, dining, and shopping.

*El Rey ruins, with the Hilton Hotel*

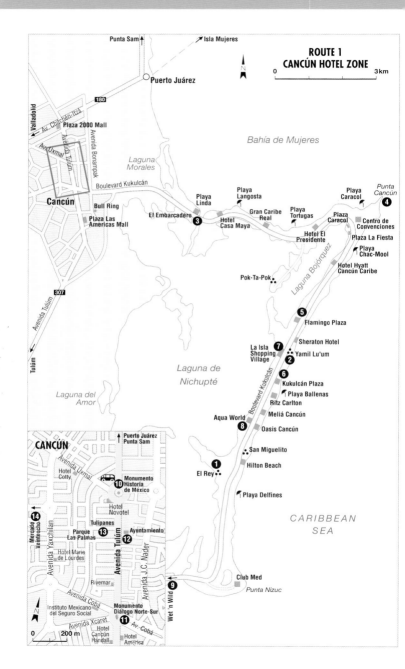

and a number of well preserved temples which still have vestiges of frescoes, as well as friezes with glyphs, numerals, and portrayals of human beings. The discovery of skeletons at El Rey suggests that it may have been a royal burial site.

A smaller site is that of **Yamil Lu'um ➋** (Km 12, overlooking the Sheraton Hotel). Here at the highest point of the island are two ruins thought to have been originally lighthouses.

## SHOPPING AND ENTERTAINMENT

A number of shopping and entertainment complexes, complete with nightclubs and restaurants, are strung out along the Boulevard. Just before the bridge at Playa Linda is the **El Embarcadero ➌**, whose attractions include the fascinating ★ **Museo de Arte Popular Mexicano**, with its colorful array of local folk art, and the **Torre Escénica**, a revolving observation tower offering great views. On Tuesdays and Fridays you can also see music and dance spectaculars performed at the **Teatro de Cancún**. The biggest concentration of activity is in the triangle of **Punta Cancún ➍**. You can shop/eat till you drop at places like the Plaza Caracol or Plaza Maya Fair and then head for some of Cancún's famous nightspots like **DadyO** or **Coco Bongo**, both at Km 9.5.

Here, too, at Km 9, is the **Cancún Convention Centre**, a striking venue for a range of cultural events and the location of the Inter Plaza, with its restaurants and boutiques, and, on the ground floor, the ★ **National Institute of Anthropology and History** (open Tues–Sun 9am–7pm); this is a small museum which traces Maya culture, with a fascinating collection of 1,000- to 1,500-year-old artefacts collected from sites throughout the province of Quintana Roo.

## LA ISLA AND OTHER HIGHLIGHTS

Heading south along the strip you have the **Flamingo Plaza** at Km 11.5 ➎ and the **Kukulcán Plaza** at Km 13 ➏, but perhaps the most enjoyable plaza of all is ★★**La Isla Shopping**

**Star Attraction**
● La Isla Shopping Village

**Best by bus**
Taxis are very expensive in Cancún, particularly for travel within the Hotel Zone. So the best and cheapest way of getting around is by bus. Regular buses ply between the Hotel Zone and downtown, and they cost just 5 pesos a ride. They stop outside all the major shopping and recreation centers and the main hotels.

*A wild time at Coco Bongo*

Map on page 24

*Below: the Aquarium at La Isla Shopping Village*
*Bottom: exploring the lagoon with AquaWorld*

Village **❼** at Km 12.5. With its themed attractions and lighting effects that make the buildings change color at night, this is the closest thing Cancún has to Las Vegas or Orlando. The stores are situated on an island, which is separated from the 'mainland' by a Venetian-style canal with bridges at strategic points.

Worth visiting here, both for adults and children, is ★★**Maya Ventura**, a gigantic maze that lets you explore the Maya world with the help of a special electronic key, picking up points as you go and learning about Maya history and culture at lively interactive displays located at each of the four 'temples' visited on the circuit. Also at La Isla is the city's latest marine attraction, the ★**Interactive Aquarium**, where visitors are 'dunked' in full diving gear into an aquarium full of tropical fish or lowered in a perspex cage to feed the sharks. During the daytime, you can also go swimming with the dolphins here.

## AQUAWORLD

Nearby is ★★**AquaWorld ❽**, which provides a host of activities for the marine enthusiast. On their Jungle Tour, drive your own 'Aqua Ray' to explore the mangroves of the Nichupté Lagoon and go out into the Caribbean for some snorkeling. You can also take to the skies aboard their

Skyrider, which is towed behind a boat in the lagoon or on the open sea; admire the wonders of the deep without getting wet aboard the *Subsee Explorer*; and learn to scuba dive – AquaWorld also offers diving excursions to the reefs off Punta Nizuc and other classic dive sites.

Finally, near the Punta Nizuc peninsula is **Parque Nizuc** with its ★ **Wet'n Wild** ❾ water park, a perfect place for kids with a variety of attractions, including the bubba tub, the kamikaze, the double-space bowl and the wave pool.

*When the crowds have gone*

## DOWNTOWN

**El Centro**, the downtown part of Cancún, reveals something of the daily Mexican routine that you simply don't see in the Hotel Zone. It was built to support the tourist industry, and this is where you will find most services, including banks, consulates, and travel agencies. Most notable about the town is the number of parks, which are well looked after and have colorful displays of local flora. They are situated in blocks either side of the main **Avenida Tulum**.

Many cities in Mexico use street intersections for monuments celebrating historical events and important figures. Cancún is no exception. The **Monumento de Historia de Mexico** ❿ towers over the traffic at Avenida Uxmal and Avenida Tulum, while the seashell-shaped **Monumento Diálogo Norte-Sur** ⓫, at Avenida Tulum and Avenida Cobá, commemorates a summit of North and South American presidents during the presidency of Luis Echeverría (1970–76).

There is a small information office situated in the colonial-style **Ayuntamiento** (town hall) ⓬, and opposite you can browse the restaurants and bars located on or around the attractively pedestrianized **Tulipanes** ⓭, which lead through to one of the many parks mentioned above. Also on Avenida Tulum, at No 17, **Ki Huic** is the largest crafts market in Cancún. If you're looking for shopping bargains, however, you'll find better prices on the parallel Avenida Yaxchilán, particularly in the enor-

Map on pages 24 & 29

**Island ferry**
If you're staying in Cancún, your hotel may well offer tours to Isla Mujeres. Depending whether you're into organized tours or not, you may want to consider the alternative, which is to take a short taxi ride to the ferry dock at **Puerto Juarez** and board the express ferry there. The ferry leaves every 30 minutes and the 15-minute crossing costs 35 pesos each way.

*The waterfront at Isla Mujeres*

mous ★ **Mercado Veinteocho** (Market 28) ⑭ Located just off Avenida Yaxchilán and Sunyax-chén, this is the hub of downtown, filled with stores and restaurants frequented by locals.

## ISLA MUJERES

Situated just to the north of Cancún, ★★★ **Isla Mujeres** is 7km (4 miles) long and only 650 meters (⅓ mile) across at its widest point. The island has a population of some 13,500, and the mainstay of the local economy is tourism, though there is also some commercial fishing.

Isla Mujeres means 'Island of Women', and there are a number of theories to account for this name. When the Spanish under Francisco Hernandez de Córdoba first arrived here in 1517, it is said that they found clay statuettes strewn along the southeastern shore, which they thought represented women. Another version states that the entire male poulation was out fishing when the Spanish landed, leading them to believe that the island was only populated by women.

There is also the tradition that the ancient Maya made pilgrimages to the island to worship Ixchel, the Moon Goddess, associated with fertility and healing. The remains of the Maya temple of Ixchel still stand at the southern tip of the island. The island was very important for the ancient Maya

Maya because it was the last place where they could find salt when en route to the Gulf of Honduras in their dug-out canoes. Salt was an indispensable element, not only to conserve the meats that were part of the Maya diet but also as an object of commerce or exchange *(see also page 12)*.

After the arrival of the Spanish, the island, with its strategic location, became a haunt for many famous pirates like Henry Morgan, El Olonés, Diego el Mulato, Lorencillo, Pata de Palo and Jean Lafitte. Stories of hidden treasures abound here. When piracy declined at the beginning of the 19th century, fishermen came here to settle and they were later joined by refugees fleeing the War of the Castes on the mainland.

**Star Attraction**
● **Isla Mujeres**

*Juice maker in Centro*

## ISLAND TOUR

Today, Isla Mujeres has a pleasant, relaxed atmosphere, a world away from Cancún. The main jetty for the ferry *(see opposite)* is at the northern end, adjacent to the main beach where all the fishing boats are hauled up. Passengers are disgorged straight into the bustling **Centro** (downtown area) **⓯**, where most of the population lives. The predominantly lowrise buildings, including a few remaining traditional clapboard houses, give the streets a distinctly Caribbean feel, and they are fun to explore. The main pedestrian thoroughfare, heading north from the market square, is **Avenida Hidalgo**. Shoppers might want to look out for some of the jewelry (gemstones, silver) for which the island is famous, as well as a wide variety of other Mexican handicrafts and textiles. There's also a good selection of restaurants, and Caribbean lobster is a particular favorite on the menus.

There are taxis, but the best ways to explore the island are on foot, by bicycle, by moped or by golf buggy, and there are plenty of people touting for your custom as you step off the ferry. Just a short walk away from downtown, reached along

Map on page 29

**Sleeping sharks**
Just off the northern tip of the island is the Shark Cave. Since sharks must be in constant motion to breathe, it shocked divers when they discovered an underwater cave in which sharks appeared to be 'sleeping'. The cave channels a natural current which allows water to pass through the sharks' gills and let them breathe while remaining immobile. The sharks can only be seen from Sept–Nov. For this and other guided diving/snorkeling excursions, we recommend you contact Sea Friends on Playa del Norte *(see page 117).*

*Turtle farm resident*

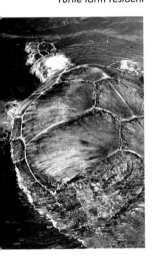

Avenida Hidalgo, is the palm-shaded ★★**Playa del Norte** ⑯. With its shallow, sheltered waters and broad white sands, this is a real paradise beach. It can get quite busy, but neither this nor the presence of the new Avalon Reef Resort on the small island of Punta Sur at the eastern extremity detract from the beauty of the place. The calm waters here are a stark contrast to the rocky east coast of the island, where it can be very rough and bathing is not recommended.

## TURTLES AND DOLPHINS

For further exploration of the island, head south along the 'main road', past the airport and between the Salina Grande and the Laguna Makax. Turn right past the tip of the lagoon and along the Carretera Sac Bajo to arrive at the ★**Isla Mujeres Turtle Farm** ⑰ (open daily 9am–5pm). Isla Mujeres is a hatching ground for the giant sea turtles who lay their eggs in the soft sand every May through September. For many years the sea turtles were killed for their meat and shell and their eggs dug up for food. They are now federally protected. The eggs are placed in pens to keep them safe from predators and the newly hatched turtles are placed in tanks until they are released into the wild by local school children.

Also on Sac Bajo is **Dolphin Discovery**, where you can swim with trained dolphins. The one-hour program features 30 minutes in the water with the dolphins and ends with a 'freestyle' swim.

## HACIENDA MUNDACA

Further south, near Playa Lancheros, is the ★**Hacienda Mundaca** ⑱ (open daily 9am–4pm), once the property of one of the island's most colorful characters, the pirate and slave trader Fermin Mundaca de Marechaja. In 1858, when the British Navy's campaign against slavery and pirates made life on the high seas too precarious, he decided to retire to Isla Mujeres. His hacienda, with its magnificent gardens, once covered more than a third of the island. He dedicated it to a local girl he had fallen in love with and whom he called *La Triguena* (the brunette); she was 18 years old at the time (37 years his junior), and so infatuated was he that he had her name carved into the entrance arches of his hacienda. But the brunette spurned his affections, instead marrying a local man by whom she had numerous children.

Mundaca ultimately died a broken man in Mérida, where he lies buried today. His empty tomb still awaits him in the Isla Mujeres cemetery. Carved by his own hands are the skull and cross bones, in memory of his pirating days, and the words meant for his love, 'As you are, I was. As I am, you will be'.

The hacienda's remaining structures, gardens and pathways have been restored and a small zoo has been added. You will see monkeys, various birds, crocodiles, pythons and even a jaguar. The best time to go to Mundaca is in the morning before it gets too hot.

## GARRAFÓN

At the southern tip of the island is the ★★ **Garrafón-Punta Sur National Park** ⓳, encompassing a rocky headland which plunges down into the great Mesoamerican Reef *(see pages 12–13)*. On the cliff top at Punta Sur, beyond the lighthouse, stand the ruins of a Maya temple dedicated

**Star Attractions**
● **Playa del Norte**
● **Garrafón**

*Below: colors of the reef*
*Bottom: Garrafón*
*Marine Park*

Map on page 29

**Cross of the Bay**

A bronze cross, almost 12 meters (39ft) high, weighing 1 ton, was mounted in the sea between the island and the mainland near the Manchones Reef in 1994. The Cross of the Bay is a tribute to the men and women who have lost their lives at sea. Thousands of divers participate in a 'mass dive' here on August 17 each year.

*Frigate bird at Isla Contoy*

to Ixchel, the Moon Goddess, and equipped with observation points which were used to make astronomical observations. Despite there being little left of the ruin itself (much of it was destroyed by Hurricane Gilbert in 1988), the fine views have not changed.

Just to the north of Punta Sur, on the west side, is the **Garrafón Marine Park**, which has been developed by the same company that runs Xcaret and Xel-Há *(see pages 37 and 39)*. You have to pay to get in, and there are gift stores, restaurants and snack bars, toilets with showers, and dive stores, all attracting more and more people to this once remote tip of the island.

The entrance fee gives you full use of the facilities (pool, sea platforms, deck chairs and palapas) as well as life vests, inner tubes, kayaks and binoculars. The most popular activity at Garrafón is snorkeling; the shallow waters above the reef here are particularly suited to beginners. Divers and snorkelers can also take a boat excursion to the main reef off Punta Sur.

## ISLA CONTOY

For a day of wildlife spotting, hop on a morning tour boat to ★★ **Isla Contoy**. The island, 24km (15 miles) northeast of Isla Mujeres, is a wildlife sanctuary and nature preserve, an important refuge of more than 90 species of aquatic and migratory birds. Only 5km (3 miles) long and 200 meters (660ft) wide, the island is a world of sand dunes, brackish lagoons and low jungle vegetation.

It gets its name from the Maya *pontoj*, meaning pelican, and in addition to brown pelicans, there are large numbers of cormorants, herons, boobies, and frigate birds, that nest in the crown of the lagoon mangroves. The fact that there is no fresh water here means that there are no mammals, so reptiles such as iguana and boa constrictors flourish. There is also a wealth of marine life, including the spiny lobster, thriving on the offshore reef; and beside the small wooden landing stage where the tour boats moor, manta rays glide fearlessly among swimmers.

# 2: The Riviera Maya

**Puerto Morelos – Xcalacoco – Playa del Carmen
– Xcaret – Akumal – Xel-Há – Tulum (– Cobá)
(131km/81 miles)**

It isn't all that long ago that the eastern coast of
the Yucatán was a virgin beach, interrupted only
by a few fishing villages and languid inlets fed by
underground rivers. Times have changed: the
backdrop of virgin jungle has been augmented by
hotel developments; villages are now towns; and
the inlets have been exploited for their touristic
appeal. That said, the Riviera Maya, as it is now
called, stretching from Cancún to Tulum, still has
miles and miles of beautiful, unspoilt beaches,
and just off the coast is the added bonus of the
Mesoamerican Reef, which provides some of the
best snorkeling and diving in the world.

There's a good variety of places to stay on the
Riviera, from popular tourist enclaves such as
Akumal and Puerto Aventuras, to the colorfully
cosmopolitan town of Playa del Carmen, to the
laid back and positively bohemian Tulum.

## PUERTO MORELOS

Increasingly, there have been moves on the part
of the local inhabitants to restrict excessive
development. This is nowhere more true than in

Map
on page
34

**Star Attraction**
● **Isla Contoy**

*Below: couple at their cabaña*
*Bottom: Playa del Carmen*

ROUTES 2 & 3

0          30 km

**Puerto Morelos**, 36km (22 miles) south of Cancún, the first port of call. The village is fortunate in the fact that it is backed by a large mangrove-filled lagoon and therefore cannot expand. This is still very much a living fishing community, and life here revolves around the shady zocalo and beyond it the fishing jetty, where you'll see fishermen mending their nets or bringing home their catch, which is served up in one of the local restaurants such as El Pescador.

It's possible to take boat trips with the fishermen to the reef that lies just offshore, and the lack of development here means that the waters are extremely clear for snorkeling and diving. Puerto Morelos is also the jumping off point for the car ferry to Cozumel *(see page 45)*, but most visitors tend to take the pedestrian only ferry from Playa del Carmen *(see below)*.

South of Puerto Morelos, look out for a dirt road that leads to **Playa del Secreto**. It used to be just that, a secret beach, very popular with the settled gringo community, but now the developers have discovered it and it's not all that secret any more. Development of a different kind can be found a little further south in the form of the ★ **Tres Ríos Tropical Reserve**. Stretching inland from a pristine mile-long white sand beach, the reserve encompasses 150 hectares (370 acres) of subtropical jungle and mangroves. You can walk or bicycle through the jungle, canoe down the river, kayak in the sea, ride a horse along the beach, snorkel in the river or at the park's reef. Scuba diving is also possible.

Further south still, there is one beach that is definitely recommended. ★★ **Xcalacoco** (follow the signs for Punta Bete) is still largely undeveloped, with just a few beach cabins and Mexican restaurants. Nearby **Punta Piedra** is even more solitary and secluded.

## PLAYA DEL CARMEN

Situated 68km (42 miles) south of Cancún, ★★ **Playa del Carmen**, or simply Playa, has grown enormously in recent years, but it still retains its

**Star Attractions**
- Xcalacoco
- Playa del Carmen

**Botanical garden**
Located right off the highway, just south of the turning for Puerto Morelos, is the Dr Alfredo Barrera Marín Botanical Gardens (open daily 9am–4pm). Covering 60 hectares (150 acres) of tropical forest, all the precious hardwoods for which Mesoamerica is famous grow here, including the chicozapote tree from which chicle (chewing gum) was and is extracted. There are collections of wild orchids, and medicinal herbs, a forest of cacti and other succulents, a chiclero camp and examples of authentic Maya housing (traditionally-made palapas). Wild deer, spider monkeys, parrots, toucans and other birds can all be spotted.

*A fresh catch at Playa*

Map on page 34

**Xaman-Há Aviary**
Situated within the Playacar development, just to the south of Playa del Carmen, this aviary (open daily 9am–5pm) is home to a representative selection of some of the exotic birds of southeastern Mexico. As well as ducks, storks, ibises and flamingos, you can see macaws, parrots and a variety of songbird species.

*The exotic toucan*

fundamental appeal as a laid-back, cosmopolitan center with a European flair. The fact that is mainly free of large resort-style hotels has made it the preferred option for many people, and local maintain that Playa, rather than Cancún, is now the center of the Yucatán's beach action. The 'locals' include a large contingent of foreigners who have settled here and set up their businesses, principally in the restaurant and bar trade.

The main hub of activity is ★★**Fifth Avenue** a pedestrian street running the length of town block behind the main beach. This is where most of the restaurants, bars and clubs are located, as well as stores selling an astonishing variety of local and foreign products. The restaurants include La Parilla, one of the best-known fish restaurants on the Riviera, Las Mañanitas with its Mexican/Italian cuisine and Palapa Hemingway which specializes in Cuban fare. If you prefer to try authentic Maya food, then head for the Yaxche; if all you want is coffee and cakes, try the Coffee Press. The verandah of the Tequila Barrel bar is a good place to sit and people-watch.

## BEACHES AND REEF

Playa would never have developed as it has were it not for the fine beaches and alluring presence of the reef just off the coast which, they say, at this point offers some of the best snorkeling and diving in the Caribbean, and is good for beginners to boot. Excursions can be arranged through any number of dive shops. The waters of the main beach itself are not as cystal clear as they used to be because of the town that has developed so much behind it, so swimming and sunbathing is best done to the north of the headland, where a chain of glorious beaches disappear into the distance (**Playa Toucan**, **Las Marmitas** and finally the famous **Coco Beach**, with its volleyball and simple palapa restaurant). At the southern side of playa's main beach is the jetty for the foot-passenger ferry to Cozumel, which comes alive in the evening due to the presence of Señor Frogs, part of the local restaurant chain.

## XCARET

Just 4km (2½ miles) to the south of Playa del Carmen is ★★★ **Xcaret** (open daily 8.30am–9.30pm). Xcaret is the Maya for 'little inlet', and for centuries the Maya settlement here, based around an inlet, was an important ceremonial center and port. Today, the natural and man-made features of Xcaret have been integrated into an eco-archeological park, with enough activites and attractions to keep you busy for a whole day.

In addition to the old Maya ruins, the 100-hectare (250-acre) site includes an aviary of exotic birds, an island with jaguars, the **Coral Reef Aquarium**, an orchid farm, a turtle farm and an enormous butterfly pavilion. Activities range from watching *papantla* flyers to relaxing on the beach; at an extra cost you can swim with the dolphins, go scuba diving, walk along the sea bed, go horse-riding or even try your hand at some game-fishing. But the most popular daytime activity – at no extra cost – is swimming along the 500-meter (1,640-ft) long ★★ **Underground River**. This is one of two rivers that flow through the site, the other being the artificially constructed but equally enticing **Maya River**, which wends its way down to the sea past a replica **Maya Village**.

The latter is one of the focal points of the park's evening entertainment program, the first half of which is devoted to various aspects of Ancient

**Star Attractions**
● **Fifth Avenue in Playa**
● **Xcaret**

*Below: the Undergound River at Xcaret*
*Bottom: Maya Ball Game participant*

Map on page 34

### Protecting the turtles

Unfortunately, growing numbers of people on Akumal's beaches at night with torches have reduced the number of successful nestings in recent years and visitors should only visit the nesting areas on a guided walk organized through the Centro Ecological Akumal at the north end of Akumal Bay. Only ten people are allowed at one time.

*Akumal apartments*

Maya culture. Things get off to a lively start with a presentation of the ★★**Maya Ball Game** *(see page 65)*, which is played in the replica ball court near the main entrance, the crowd cheering whenever a 'warrior' succeeds in propelling the latex ball through one of the rings. Afterwards, small groups are led to the Maya Village and its adjoining caves for performances of a number of rituals, including ceremonies involving shamans and the Owl Man. Then comes the grand finale, the **Folkloric Show** held at the spectacular open-air amphitheater, at which hundreds of colorfully costumed artists perform traditional music, song and dance from the different Mexican states.

## SOUTH TO AKUMAL

South of Xcaret is the port facility at **Calica**, which serves Caribbean cruise ships. Beyond that lie a string of coastal resorts, starting with **Puerto Aventuras**, a modern development created around a marina. To the south is **Xpu-Ha** beach, with its beautiful white sand, but no longer quite so secluded since development arrived here in the shape of the Palace Resort.

★**Akumal**, meaning 'place of the turtles', lies 37km (23 miles) south of Playa del Carmen. Begun as an exclusive resort for scuba divers way back in the 1950s, it has grown considerably since but is still a relaxing place to be. There are two main bays, Akumal Bay and Half Moon Bay, both protected by the reef and offering excellent snorkeling (with lots of brain coral in the middle of Half Moon Bay). Just to the north, swimmers and snorkelers can also enjoy the Yal Kú lagoon.

But as its name suggests, Akumal is best known as a nesting ground for the giant sea turtles which come ashore here between May and November *(see box)*. While out diving or snorkeling, stay clear of any turtles you see, so as not to disturb their natural feeding patterns.

Turtles also come ashore to nest at ★**Xcacel Beach** to the south of Akumal. This is one of the most beautiful beaches on the coast, but it too is under siege by large-scale resort development.

## AKTUN CHEN

Three kilometers (2 miles) south of Akumal are the ★**Aktun Chen caves**. Aktun Chen means 'cave with an cenote inside', and there is a total of three caves here. The main one is 550 meters (600 yards) long, with a magnificent vault.

Illuminated paths have been created for easy walking among the thousands of stalactites, stalagmites, and a crystal-clear cenote that is over 12 meters (40ft) deep. Trained guides accompany visitors, providing a combined history lesson and geology class.

Surrounding the caves is the jungle, with special trails that provide a look at the local wildlife, including white-tailed deer, spider monkeys, iguana, and wild turkey.

**Star Attractions**
- Maya Ball Game
- Xel-Há

*Below: resident of the cenote at Xel-Há*
*Bottom: snorkeling down the inlet*

## XEL-HÁ

Almost as popular as Xcaret is the ecopark of ★★★**Xel-Há**. Meaning 'the place where water is born' in Maya, the park is centered on a large natural inlet fed by the area's underground river system; with open access to the sea, its waters are a combination of salt water and fresh water, creating an extraordinary natural aquarium. In pre-Hispanic times, this was an important commercial harbor, and it is said that Maya gods gave Xel-Há to mortals, and the place was guarded by two

Map on page 34

*Below: getting around*
*Xel-Há by bike*
*Bottom: a rough afternoon at*
*the promontory*

Maya symbols, the parrot fish signifying illusion and love, and the iguana representing wisdom. There are still plenty of parrot fish here, and iguana are easily spotted next to the jungle trails.

You can either walk or take the 'train' to the headwaters, and then snorkel or float with the current on an inner tube down the inlet, admiring the fish and coral on the way. Note that the further toward the sea you get, the bigger the fish, and you can even see barracudas in the lower reaches. Landlubbers can hike through the jungle to visit the two cenotes on the site; other attractions include a Maya cave and an archeological zone. Facilities (restaurants, stores and changing rooms for snorkelers) are all located on the north side of the inlet, and from here there is a pleasant walk down to the promontory with its lighthouse and natural pool. Near the entrance is a large pool where you can swim with dolphins.

## ANCIENT XEL-HÁ

Take a break from the water and cross the highway to visit the Maya site of ★ **Xel-Há** (open daily 8am–5pm). These ruins are some of the oldest on the peninsula, dating back to the late Pre-Classic period (from around AD100), although the site reached its peak in Post-Classic times (AD900–1500), when Xel-Há functioned as a port and

trading station, and probably as an embarkation point for crossings to Cozumel. Of particular note is ★ **Templo de los Pajaros** (Bird Temple) belonging to the Early Classic period (AD200–600). Unfortunately, the temple was partially destroyed when the highway was built in the 1970s, but a fresco depicting some of the region's birds remains. Chac (the god of rain) is also represented here. Another highlight, in a different part of the site, and reached along a 500-m (550-yard) long *sacbé* (raised causeway) is the **Casa del Jaguar** (the House of the Jaguar), named after the painting of a descending jaguar.

Also well worth seeing is the site's very own cenote. This area has the highest concentration of cenotes on the coast, and it is possible to explore some of these underground wonders further by visiting the ★★★ **Hidden Worlds Cenotes**, located to the south of Xel-Ha just to the west of Highway 307 *(see box)*.

## TULUM

Perched on a low cliff above the powdery white sands and turquoise waters of the Caribbean, and backed by lush vegetation, the Maya city of ★★★ **Tulum** (open daily, summer 8am–7pm, winter 7am–6pm) boasts the most spectacular location of any ruins on the peninsula. It is the overall dramatic effect, rather than any detail of the ruins themselves, that draws large numbers of visitors to this site; in truth, Tulum was never more than a relatively minor provincial outpost, a trading center that only reached its heyday in the Post Classic period (around AD1200), after the Maya world had disintegrated into warring states. It was first spotted by Juan de Grijalva and his men as they reconnoitred the eastern coast of Yucatán in 1518; when it was conquered by the Spanish in 1530, Tulum was still a thriving city.

The Maya name 'Tulum' means wall, and one unusual feature of the site is that it is surrounded by a wall, which was probably used for defensive purposes. However, the majority of residents would have lived outside this perimeter, the inner

**Star Attractions**
● **Hidden Worlds Cenotes**
● **Tulum**

**Hidden Worlds**
Hidden Worlds Cenotes (snorkel and diving tours daily at 9am, 11am and 1pm) is the world's largest cavern diving and snorkeling complex, and whether you're a novice snorkeler or a certified diver, it's an absolute must. The tours take you through the jungle to some awesome caverns and cenotes with crystal clear water and stalactite formations, including the Dos Ojos cenote and the Bat Cave. These and other caverns are part of a massive underground system that provides some of the best cavern diving anywhere on the planet.

*The Castillo at Tulum*

Map on page 34

**Queen of Tulum**
During the Maya uprising known as the War of the Castes (1847–1901), Tulum served as a fortress for the rebels. In 1871, it was used as a sanctuary by the cult of the 'Talking Cross' of Chan Santa Cruz. They were led by Maria Uicab, an indigenous Maya woman, whose bravery and determination earned her the title of Queen of Tulum.

*The Temple of Frescoes*

sanctum being reserved for the ruling classes. Even at its height, Tulum's population was never more than about 600.

## HIGHLIGHTS

The city's original name was *Zama* or Dawn, thought to refer to its location facing the rising sun. Directly overlooking the sea, the most dominant building is the so-called **Castillo**, which is thought to have functioned as a lighthouse as well as a temple. Braced against the elements, there are only a few narrow openings on the seaward side. On the landward side, notice the two columns with lintels portraying plumed serpents, a clear indication of Toltec influence.

To the left of the platform at the base of the Castillo is the **Temple of the Descending God**. The small, upside-down figure of the diving or descending god depicted above the narrow entrance of the temple appears all over Tulum. His exact significance is not known; he may represent the setting sun, rain, lightning, or he may be the Bee God, since honey was – and still is – one of the Maya's most important exports.

Situated near the entrance, the **Temple of Frescoes** is another interesting building, with columns on the bottom level and a smaller room on the top. The frescoes here, now mostly erased by the elements, include one of human figures in the Toltec style. Bas-reliefs of Chac, the Maya god of rain, extend around the corners of the main lintel and facade.

The walled part of the city covers only a small part of what can be explored at Tulum, which occupies a 650-hectare (1,600-acre) national park stretching north and south of the site. The small bay just to the north of the Castillo may well have been the dock for trading ships. On a promontory just to the north is a small single-roomed structure called the **Temple of the Wind**, an apt description for any building in this exposed site. There are fantastic views from here, as there are from a similar structure called the **Temple of the Sea** at the southern edge of the site.

## ALONG THE BOCA PAILA ROAD

The ruins are only one aspect of Tulum. There is also a small town which straddles Highway 307, where restaurants, banks and a host of other services are located. And to the south, along the coast road (Boca Paila Road), is a series of beautiful beaches. The fact that there is little in the way of resort development here is indicative of the laid-back, Bohemian atmosphere of Tulum. Budget travelers usually head for the cheap cabañas on the beach just south of the ruins, but there are other, really attractive options further along, including a number of guesthouses on their own ★★**idyllic bays**.

The Boca Paila Road continues south to the hamlet of Boca Paila, and then along a narrow spit at the end of which lies the village of **Punta Allen**; this small fishing community is one of the bases for exploring the ★★**Sian Ka'an Biosphere Reserve**, with its reef and lagoons and fantastic array of wildlife *(see page 12)*. There are a number of firms and private individuals based here offering trips into the nearby Black Lagoon with its mangroves, as well as to the reef for diving and snorkeling. Fly-fishing is also popular.

However, visitors should note that due to its exposed position on a narrow spit of land, the road to Punta Allen is in a poor state of repair. Because of the deep ruts, you are advised to take a four-

**Star Attractions**
● **bays south of Tulum**
● **Sian Ka'an Biosphere Reserve**

*Below: palm-fringed beach south of the ruins*
*Bottom: amenities on the Boca Paila Road*

Map on page 34

**Maya roads**

Now mostly hidden by jungle, the elevated roads or causeways that connected Maya cities were between 3 and 20 meters (10 and 65ft) wide and were covered with limestone plaster, hence their name *sacbeob* (Maya for white roads). Their purpose is puzzling as the Maya had no wheeled transport and had yet to see the horse, but they may have been built for religious processions and pilgrimages. No less than 50 such roads converged on Cobá.

*Cobá's Nohoch Mul pyramid*

wheel drive rather than a standard car. The potholes can fill up with rainwater and make driving hazardous, but whatever the conditions you should allow at least 2 hours for the 50-km (30-mile) trip.

## DETOUR TO COBÁ

The Maya city of ★★ **Cobá** (open daily 8am–7pm in summer, 7am–6pm in winter) lies 40km (25 miles) northeast of Tulum, along a ruler-straight, if often potholed, road that eventually links up with Highway 180 near Valladolid. Cobá, meaning 'water stirred by the wind', is set among a small lake system, and it is the presence of water that might account for the site having thrived for so long – for over a thousand years from the Early Classic period onwards. Cobá, which reached its height in the 9th century, was a powerful regional player and also a hub of a Maya road network: one *sacbe* (elevated road) linked it with Yaxuná in central Yucatán, 97km (60 miles) away.

The site covers a vast area. There are said to be some 6,000 buildings here, but only a small proportion have been excavated. The Cobá group near the entrance includes the **Iglesia Pyramid**, whose rounded corners are a distinctive feature, as well as a superbly restored **Ball Court**; though much smaller than the one at Chichén Itzá, the latter is still a fine example of this typical feature of the larger Maya sites.

The main attraction, however, is the enormous ★★ **Nohoch Mul pyramid** in the group of the same name. All of 42 meters (138ft) high, this is the tallest structure in the northern Yucatán. The views of the jungle and lakes from the top are superb. The pyramid's slenderness and steepness is reminiscent of those further south, such as at Calakmul *(see page 98)* and at Tikal in Guatamala, and there could well have been close contact between all these cities.

Of further interest are the **stelae** found at the **Macanxoc group** to the east of the lake of the same name. The figures carved into the stelae depict royal women standing on the heads of their helpless captives.

# 3: Cozumel

Lying just off the coast of the Riviera Maya, and easily accessible by passenger ferry from Playa del Carmen, is the island of Cozumel. With a length of 48km (30 miles) and maximum width of 16km (10 miles), it is Mexico's largest island. Its 30km (18 miles) of white sandy beaches have made Cozumel today a paradise for sun-worshipers, but the island is perhaps most famous for the reefs that lie off its western shore, which provide superb coral diving.

Map on page 34

**Star Attraction**
● Cobá

## ISLAND OF SWALLOWS

Unlike visitors today, the ancient Maya of Cozumel did not worship the sun but the fertilty goddess, Ixchel. As was the case with Isla Mujeres *(see page 28)*, women would travel here seeking her divine intervention. According to legend, Ixchel acknowledged the shrines and temples built in her honor by sending her favorite bird, the swallow. Thus the island was named *Cuzamil,* 'Land of swallows'.

It was predicted in the *Chilam Balam* – Maya history books – that bearded conquerors would one day come from the east, and thus the natives were hardly surprised when Cortés and his fellow conquistadors landed on Cozumel in 1519, before

*Below: San Miguel visitor*
*Bottom: underwater paradise*

Map on page 34

### Getting around
Traveling around Cozumel couldn't be easier. The island is almost encircled by a coastal road, the Costera Sur, and running across the middle, between San Miguel and the east coast, is the Carretera Transversal. The only coastal parts of the island to which access is limited are the northwest and southern tips, both havens for birds and other wildlife. The best way of getting around is by hire car or moped, but it's also possible to take a taxi.

*Ready for the road*

heading onward up the coast of Mexico. After the arrival of the Spanish, the poulation was decimated by disease, and by the 19th century the island had become almost uninhabited, being recolonized by Maya from the Talking Cross sect only after the mid-century War of the Castes.

Little by little the population grew, partially because of the world demand for chewing-gum, the raw material for which, chicle, was harvested from local trees. There was a limited amount of tourism in the early part of the 20th century, but the island remained a relatively sleepy backwater, and it was only when the French underwater explorer Jacques Cousteau explored and filmed the Palancar Reef in the early 1960s that the wonders of Cozumel came to the attention of the world at large. This and the subsequent development of Cancún provided the catalyst for a boom that has converted the island into a magnet for international tourists.

## SAN MIGUEL DE COZUMEL

If you're arriving by passenger ferry from Playa del Carmen, your first port of call on Cozumel will be the island's only big settlement, the capital **San Miguel de Cozumel**. Once a small fishing town, San Miguel is an attractive, lively place, with smart stores and a whole range of top quality restaurants and watering holes along its pedestrianized streets. In the central **Plaza del Sol**, where local musicians perform on Sunday evenings, are statues to revolutionary leader Benito Juarez and General Andrés Quintana Roo. Running along the seafront is the busy Avenida Rafael Melgar, also known as the **Malecón**, with outlets for all kinds of merchandise. Loose gemstones and jewelry are a big thing here, with famous-name and less well known diamond merchants, each with a sign welcoming passengers from that day's visiting cruise ships.

Along the same street, a couple of blocks north of the ferry dock, is the ★ **Museo de la Isla de Cozumel** (open daily 10am–6pm). Housed in an attractive old building that was originally the first luxury hotel on the island, opened in 1936, the museum has well designed exhibits providing full coverage of the island's history, both natural and cultural, explaining, for instance, how coral is formed and illustrating the local flora and fauna. Upstairs are pieces from both the pre-Hispanic and Spanish colonial eras, and there is a room dedicated to the families who settled in Cozumel in the 19th century after the War of the Castes. A pleasant terrace café, El Museo, offers ocean views.

**Star Attraction**
● Chankanaab State Park

## HEADING SOUTH

To explore the coast of Cozumel, follow the Costera Sur south of the capital, passing after 3km (2 miles) the new cruise ship terminal at **La Ceiba**. The construction of the berth caused outrage among environmentalists and divers because it destroyed the North Paradise Reef.

Two kilometers further on is the entrance to the ★★ **Chankanaab State Park**, which is almost worth a full day to itself. Less developed than Xcaret and Xel-Ha *(see pages 37 and 39)*, this ecopark, with its glorious beaches, is centered on a crystal clear lagoon (the name means 'small sea'). The lagoon itself is just for swimming, but you can go reef diving and snorkeling offshore. The top attraction is the **Swim with Dolphins** program, probably the best in the Yucatán, but there's

*Below: parrots at Chankanaab, where you can also swim with the dolphins (bottom)*

Map on page 34

**Protected reefs**
For the dazzling variety and beauty of their underwater flora and fauna, the reefs of Cozumel deserve their reputation as among the best in the world. Also contributing to their popularity is their easy access and year-round clear water. More than 80 percent of the reefs are now protected within the Cozumel Reefs National Park, which was created in 1996. There is a small daily charge for diving in the park.

*Preparations at Cozumel Beach Park*

also a **Botanical Garden** surrounding the lagoon, and an **Archeological Park** which contains reproductions of artefacts from Olmec, Maya, Toltec and Aztec cultures.

## REEFS AND BEACHES

Offshore to the south of Chankanaab lie the majority of the island's famous reefs, including the best known of all, the **Palancar Reef**, with its giant canyons of coral dropping to the ocean depths. But non-divers will not be disappointed by this stretch of coast, which includes the palm-fringed beaches of Playa San Francisco, Playa del Sol and Playa de Palancar. The ★ **Cozumel Beach Park** at Playa del Sol has a restaurant and freshwater pool as well as a small zoo with animals indigenous to the Yucatán; there is also the underwater and rather surreal **Maya City** for divers and snorkelers, which incorporates various replica structures and sculptural features of the Maya world, from plumed serpents to reclining Chac-Mools.

## TO PUNTA SUR

Between Playa del Sol and Playa de Palancar you will see a dirt road marked by an arch and leading to the settlement of ★ **El Cedral** and its Maya ruins (open daily 8am–5pm), hidden deep in the jungle. It was in El Cedral that the first Catholic mass in Mexico was held, on 6 May, 1518. In May each year the settlement re-enacts the event and also holds a colorful fiesta.

The very southern part of the island is protected by the ★★ **Punta Sur Ecological Reserve**, which encompasses the wild beaches and dunes of the coast, plus interior lagoons and mangrove swamps, all havens to a rich diversity of birds, reptiles, fish and vegetation. Access is not permitted by car, but buggies and bicycles are provided, and there are observation towers and walkways. The park incorporates the southernmost point of the island, Punta Celarain, where the ★ **Punta Celarain Lighthouse** has been restored to house a Museum of Navigation.

## THE EAST COAST

From Punta Sur, the Costera Sur heads north along the east coast. With its exposed, rocky shore, this side of the island is a complete contrast to the sheltered west coast. There are some secluded beaches, but these are mostly deserted and swimming is not recommended because of the dangerous undertow. Other than a few farms, there is little development until you reach **Punta Morena** with its bar and souvenir stand.

Ignore for the moment the Carretera Transversal which crosses the island back to San Miguel, and continue up the coast until a turning on the left leads to the Maya ruins of ★ **San Gervasio** (open daily 8am–5pm). Though not particularly impressive when compared to sites on the mainland, San Gervasio is famous for its sanctuary of the Maya goddess of fertility, Ixchel. In ancient times pilgrims made their way here from as far away as central Mexico to leave offerings to the goddess; it is said that a priest would hide behind a statue and, like a ventriloquist, answer the pilgrims' supplications as the voice of the goddess. This Classic Maya tradition lived on in the Cult of the Talking Cross *(see pages 16 and 42)*, which grew up in the 19th century after the War of the Castes, when the Maya rebels sought refuge in the jungle of Quintana Roo and on the islands of Cozumel and Isla Mujeres.

**Star Attraction**
● **Punta Sur Ecological Reserve**

*Below: warden with wild pig and (bottom) the protected coast at Punta Sur*

Map below

*Valladolid cathedral*

# 4: Cancún to Mérida

**Cancún – Valladolid – (Río Lagartos) – Balancanché Caves – Chichén Itzá – Izamal – Aké – Mérida (318km/197 miles)**

This route leaves Cancún and the Riviera Maya behind to explore some of the sights of the northern Yucatán. A toll motorway *(cuota)* covers most of the distance between Cancún and Mérida, but if you want to take your time, it's definitely more interesting to take Highway 180, which is accessed by leaving downtown Cancún along Avenida Uzmal. There are Maya cities and colonial towns along the way, and you can also strike out to explore some of the Yucatán's north coast.

Most of the places described on this route can be reached by public transport, but renting a car gives you the freedom to explore the rural interior. By far the best known destination along Highway 180 is the great Maya/Toltec city of Chichén Itzá, which is described in detail in the next chapter. Travelers not going as far as Mérida can do an interesting circuit by returning from there to the Riviera at Tulum via Cobá *(see page 44)*.

Almost as soon as you leave Cancún behind, you enter a different world. No great wealth and blitz here as you enter the real Yucatán, a landscape swathed in *monte* (jungle), as locals call it, and peppered with *milpas*, the fecund plots in which Maya farmers raise their crops of corn, beans, chilies, sweet potato and melons.

As you pass through towns such as **Leona Vicrio** and **Nuevo Xcán**, in amongst new concrete dwellings you'll see plenty of the traditional Maya houses, with their walls of wooden poles, roofs of thatched palm and typically rounded corners. As cars pass, savvy peddlars with fruit or figurines hang out beside the ubiquitous *topes* (speed bumps) to try and make a sale.

## VALLADOLID

Around 160km (100 miles) from Cancún on Highway 180, the city of ★★ **Valladolid** stands on the ancient Maya ceremonial center of Zací. When the Spanish conquistadors began their invasion of the peninsula, towns like this one were built quickly to enforce the new European culture

**Star Attraction**
● **Valladolid**

**Isla Holbox**
At the far northeastern corner of the Yucatán peninsula, separated from the mainland by the Yalahua Lagoon, is Isla Holbox. Much less developed than the Riviera resorts, this is a perfect place to get away from it all. The village of Holbox, with its sandy streets and wooden houses, is still inhabited mostly by fishermen and their families. The island has fine sandy beaches strewn with shells, and is also a great place for birdwatching. To get there turn off Highway 180 at El Ideal for Chiquilá, and from there take the ferry (crossings at 6, 8 & 10am, noon, 4 & 5pm).

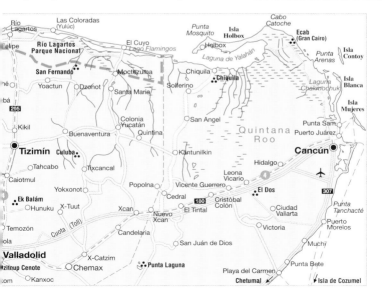

Map
on pages
50–1

*Below: refreshments at
the Convent of San
Bernardino of Siena
Bottom: Valladolid's
central plaza*

and religion on the local indigenous population
Today, many of the city's fine colonial mansion
have been painstakingly restored in their origina
hues, and there are a number of interestin
churches to visit.

## SIGHTS AND CENOTES

Life in Valladolid revolves around the centra
plaza. Along the north side, Maya women in the
traditional *huipil* dresses congregate daily to se
clothes and handicrafts. The shady plaza itsel
is a good place to relax in the shade of the brigh
yellow *czarena* trees. On the south side of th
Square is the **Cathedral of San Gervasio**. Con
secrated in 1545, it later had to be rebuilt becaus
of 'crimes commited on the main altar'. It is con
sidered a punished church as its main entranc
now faces north rather than east.

In the southwest part of the town, at the en
of the attractive Calle 41A, is Valladolid's mos
impressive monument, the **★★ Convent of Sa
Bernardino of Siena**. Begun in 1552, under th
direction of the Franciscan Friar Juan de Mérid
this was the first convent to be constructed i
the Americas and played an important role i
proselytizing the Maya. This massive, squa
building wears the patina of ages, but you can sti
see some of the original frescoes behind the sid

altars. The other main church in Valladolid is the Cathedral of Santa Lucia in the north of the town, at the corner of Calle 40 and Calle 27.

Well worth a visit – and even more so if you can read the Spanish explanations – is the ★ **Museo San Roque**, just east of the central plaza on Calle 41. Housed in a converted chapel, it contains exhibits of Maya arts and crafts made in the surrounding villages, as well as finds from the archeological excavations at Ek Balam *(see below)*. There are also tableaux devoted to the War of the Castes (1847–1901), when Valladolid was taken over by Maya rebels *(see box)*.

For an insight into local Maya life today, visit the lively **Municipal Market** to the east of the town center. Predominantly a food market, set around a central arcaded hall, it's a good place to stock up on fruit and other supplies.

On the way to the market, you'll pass **Cenote Zací**, one of the town's two cenotes. It's not possible to swim here because the water is too murky, but it's a nice walk around the edge, and there's a small aviary near the entrance. The cenote was used as a hiding place by local rebels during the uprising. The other cenote is the ★ **Dzitnup** (or Xkeken) cenote, just off Highway 180 about 4km (2½ miles) to the west of town, and its cavernous interior is a great place for a refreshing dip.

## EK BALAM

Highway 295 heads due north for 101km (63 miles) to the small coastal town of Río Lagartos. But don't head straight there, because just off the main road there's an extraordinary Maya site to visit. Fifteen kilometers (9 miles) north of Valladolid, look out for the turning to Ek Balam, and follow the narrow country lane for another 10km (6 miles) until you reach the site.

Wrested from the jungle relatively recently, ★★ **Ek Balam** (open daily 8am–5pm) is one of the most impressive Maya sites in the Yucatán. This isn't just on account of the wonderful restoration that has taken place, but also because of the sheer scale of the buildings. Ek Balam, which

**Star Attractions**
● Convent of San Bernardino of Siena
● Ek Balam

**Valladolid Uprising**
Nowhere was the carnage of the War of the Castes *(see pages 16 and 19)* greater than in Valladolid. The city was a bastion of racism and exploitation, where Maya and mestizos were banned from the main plaza and the smarter streets. On 19 January 1847, 15,000 Maya warriors stormed in. There were hundreds of deaths, but the uprising ended as abruptly as it had begun when the Maya – reminded of their rural obligations by the annual sighting of the winged ant – returned to their fields to plant the year's corn.

*The Dzitnup cenote*

**Map on pages 50–1**

### The Gate of Hell

The main frieze at Ek Balam is a masterful representation of Itzamná, the God of Creation or 'Earth Monster'. The dark entrance is the monster's mouth, complete with a fearsome set of teeth. On the nose above sits a cross-legged deity, and small statues sitting in the eye sockets survey the city. To the right and left are life-size statues of the city's rulers. Behind the entrance, the 'Gate of Hell', is a 6-meter (20-ft) drop, and it is thought that the rulers disposed of their prisoners here – they were simply thrown into the void and impaled on spikes at the bottom.

*Frieze detail, Ek Balam*

means 'black jaguar' in Maya, is thought to have reached its height between AD700–1000. It is spread over a wide area, though the main structures cover just one square kilometer. They are surrounded by two stone walls (thought to have been built for social demarcation rather than any military purpose) and are centered around two connecting spaces called the Central and Southern Plazas, with the Ball Court in between. Wherever you stand at Ek Balam, your gaze is drawn to the main pyramid at the north end of the site.

All of 160 meters (525ft) wide, 75 meters (250ft) deep and 31 meters (100ft) high, the so-called ★★★ **Acropolis** is an enormous structure. And as you climb to the top you'll see that this is no 'ordinary' pyramid: there are platforms and tunnels running in all directions; and under the big canopy to the left of the main steps is a massive 6.5-meter (20-ft) high wall sporting one of the most elaborate ★★★ **decorative friezes** ever discovered in the Maya world (*see box*).

The ★★ **view** from the top is magnificent. To the left and right are Ek Balam's two other pyramids that have not yet been restored, cloaked in vegetation; beyond the ruins, the Yucatán jungle stretches away to an empty horizon, only punctuated some 50km (32 miles) to the southeast by the giant Nohoch Mul pyramid of Cobá, and at a similar distance to the southwest by the Castillo of Chichén Itzá. It is astonishing to think that, after all this time, the only landmarks visible are the pyramids of ancient cities.

## RIO LAGARTOS

Highway 295 continues via the busy town of Tizimín and across the flat landscape of the northern Yucatán to arrive finally at the little coastal town of **Río Lagartos**. Still largely untouched by mass tourism, this is very much a fishing community, and the flat-bottomed fishing boats are lined up along the waterfront. Named 'Crocodile River' by the Spaniards for the alligators that once infested the area but are now less common, Río Lagartos is situated on the landward side of a large lagoon which extends all the way from San Felipe in the west to El Cayo in the east. The lagoon and the long spit of land enclosing it together form the ★★ **Río Lagartos National Park**. Founded in 1979, this reserve has a large pink flamingo population, and is home to some 200 further bird species including the frigate, snowy egret, red egret, white ibis and blue heron. The park is also home to the giant salt works at **Las Coloradas** *(see page 12)*.

## A BIRDWATCHER'S PARADISE

Local guides (for contacts, *see page 118*) operate boat excursions for tourists, and for around 400 pesos they will take you on a tour of the park to see the flamingos, which are resident all year round. This involves following channels through the extensive mangroves that skirt the lagoon, and it is an experience not to be missed, for the birdlife is truly amazing. For serious birdwatchers, boat trips can be combined with jungle walks. Night-time crocodile-spotting tours are also possible.

The guides are experts on the local flora and fauna; they'll explain to you the difference between a red and a black mangrove and even point out a horseshoe crab lurking in the shallower parts of the lagoon. The horseshoe crab *(cacarola de mar)* has evolved little since it first appeared on earth hundreds of millions of years ago.

**Star Attractions**
● **Ek Balam's Acropolis**
● **Río Lagartos National Park**

*Below: a horseshoe crab at Río Lagartos*
*Bottom: the waterfront and lagoon, Río Lagartos*

**Map on pages 50–1**

**Ik Kil cenote**
If you're hot and tired after a long car or bus ride, why not stop at the **Ik Kil cenote**, just 2km (1 mile) before Chichén Itzá. Though the entrance fee is quite steep, this is a great place for a cool swim. The cenote is open to the sky with waterfalls and jungle creepers overhead. There is cabaña accommodation available, and a pleasant restaurant set in lush gardens.

*Ceremonial objects at the Balancanché caves*

Return along the 295 to Valladolid, and from there continue the westward journey toward Mérida along Highway 180. The increasing presence of large roadside stalls selling handicrafts indicate that we are now getting close to Chichén Itzá. A detailed tour of the site itself is described in the following chapter, but there is one other sight in the vicinity that merits attention.

## GRUTAS DE BALANCANCHE

In 1959, a Chichén Itzá tour guide, while surveying the area, stumbled upon the ★★ **Balancanché Caves** (open daily 9am– 5pm), 6km (4 miles) from Chichén Itzá along Highway 180. He found a hidden passage leading underground through a series of caverns, ending in an enormous circular chamber bristling with stalactites and with a huge stalagmite rising like a column in the middle. Around its base were ceremonial objects and offerings to the rain god, Tlaloc (the Toltecs' image of the Maya god, Chac), that had been left here 800 years previously by the ancient Maya. Most of the artefacts are in the same place as they were found. Self-guided tours (in Spanish at 9am, noon, 2pm and 4pm; English at 11am, 1pm and 3pm) are synchronized with commentary, and a music and light show.

In the visitors' center there's an interesting ★ **museum** that tells you more about Balancanché and local Maya beliefs. The last rain ceremony to take place at Balancanché was in 1988, but in the surrounding villages the Maya still conduct their rain cermeonies during times of drought.

## IZAMAL

Continue west on Highway 180, past the entrance to Chichén Itzá *(see page 60)*, and on through gently undulating country for another 40km (25 miles) or so to Kantunil. Turn right off the main road here for ★★★ **Izamal**. There is nowhere else in the Yucatán where the interface between Maya and colonial history is so visible as in Izamal. With its huge convent, churches and mansions

Izamal, the 'city of the hills', wears the garb of a colonial town, but before the Spanish arrived this was a large and prosperous Maya city, occupied continuously from the late Pre-Classic period onwards (from about 300BC). The hills refer to the Maya pyramids that are still part of the townscape today.

## POWERS OF HEALING

Izamal was dedicated to the worship of Itzamná, who was patron of learning, science, and the arts, and also associated with healing and medicine. Already established as a major pilgrimage center for the Maya, it was converted to a Christian pilgrimage site by the Franciscan order after they arrived in 1549, under the leadership of none other than Fra Diego de Landa, bishop of the Yucatán and the man responsible for the auto-da-fé, the burning of the Maya books at Maní *(see page 79)*.

The local Maya were forced to dismantle the Popul Chac pyramid in the center of their city, and over its base the Spanish constructed an enormous convent, in which they installed their own miracle-working icon, a wooden statue of the Virgin Mary. Completed between 1554 and 1618, the ★★ **Convento de San Antonio de Padua** is the largest monastery in the region; its atrium, with 75 arches, is claimed to be the largest in the world

**Star Attractions**
● **Balancché caves**
● **Izamal and the Convento de San Antonio de Padua**

*Below: atrium of Izamal's Convento de San Antonio de Padua*
*Bottom: calesas on the plaza*

**Map on pages 50–1**

**The color yellow**
Painting the whole of Izamal yellow is a tradition said to have been started by a colonial governor of the town. Perhaps it was done in deference to the local Maya, for yellow is the color of corn and for the Maya corn was the symbol of life itself.

*Izamal's town hall*

after St Peter's, Rome. The church is most interesting for its frescoes, depicting key events and stories from Christianity as related to the indigenous population. The Virgin of Izamal, one of the most venerated Christian icons in the Yucatán, is celebrated with a lavish festival of music and dance on August 15, and again during a week-long festival in early December.

The town itself fans out from the two central plazas adjacent to the convent, and it is a very attractive place with its largely single-story mansions. A notable feature of Izamal is that all its buildings are painted in the same yellow color, lending the streets a striking air of uniformity *(see box)*. The town is easy to explore on foot, but you can also take a horse-drawn carriage *(calesa)*.

Of the Maya pyramids still standing in Izamal today, by far the largest and most complete is that of ★★ **Kinich Kakmo** (open daily 8am–5pm), just three blocks north of the convent and the main plaza. Covering an entire block almost 200 meters (650ft) square, this is the largest known structure of the entire Maya world. There is a smaller pyramid on top of the base, and when you get to the top the views of the town and surrounding countryside are superb. From this vantage point you realize just how large the convent is as well.

## AKÉ

From Izamal you can either return to Highway 180 via the small town of **Hóctun**, or take minor back roads to Mérida. The latter option involves passing through Citilcum, Tekanto, Bokoba and Cacalchén before arriving at the small Maya village of ★ **Aké**, which has several points of interest, though few tourists seem to make it here.

Firstly, there is the ancient Maya city of Aké, which was already an important site in the area before AD300; it is thought that local leaders met here to plan alliances. The ancient city was connected with nearby Izamal by a 31-km (19-mile) sacbé (elevated Maya road). The most notable feature of the ruins (open daily 8am–5pm) is the huge palace or Acropolis, which is ascended by a 46-meter (150-ft) wide stairway of 27 steps, and topped with 36 stone pillars which once supported a wooden roof. The Acropolis is distinctive for its use of massive limestone blocks rather than smaller stones.

Adjacent to the ruins is an old henequen factory, part of which is still in operation, and for a fee of 30 pesos you can go in and watch men and machinery at work. There is still a large modern Maya community at Aké, living and working the land in the same style as their ancient ancestors, as well as turning out all manner of handicrafts.

**Star Attraction**
● **Kinich Kakmo in Izamel**

## HACIENDAS

The landscape between Aké and Merida is dotted with ex-henequen haciendas. Some have been converted into hotels, but are still worth a stop. They include the ★ **Hacienda Katanchel** just off Highway 180 (take the road south from Tixpehual just beyond Aké). Converted into a luxury hotel, complete with pool, lush gardens, bar, restaurant and billiard room, Katanchel is also open to non-residents. Less exclusive, and popular with locals for weddings and other functions, is the **Teya Hacienda** (just off Highway 180, 12.5km/8 miles from Mérida), whose well-kept gardens create a colorful oasis in the midst of henequen fields. The restaurant here offers authentic Yucatecan cuisine.

*Below: Maya column and old hacienda at Aké*
*Bottom: Hacienda Katanchel*

Map on pages 50–1, 62

*Below: serpent at the Ball Court*
*Bottom: the Kukulcán Pyramid, Chichén Itzá's dominant structure*

# 5: Chichén Itzá

Situated on Highway 180, 116km (72 miles) from Mérida and 180km (112 miles) from Cancún, ★★★ **Chichén Itzá** (open daily 8am–5pm) is the best known and most spectacular Maya site in the whole of the Yucatán. Plan to spend at least a whole day here, and if you want to stay overnight, there are two fine hotels near the southern section of the site. For more economical accommodation, try the nearby town of Pisté.

The entrance ticket allows you to enter and leave the site as often as you wish on the same day; it also covers attendance at the impressive **Light and Sound** show, which takes place in the evening (daily except Sun, 7pm in winter, 8pm in summer; translation available through headset).

## MAYA AND TOLTEC

The name Chichén Itzá means 'Mouth of the Itza Wells', referring to the two local cenotes (one of which supplied the city with its water, the other being reserved for sacrificial rituals), and the Itzá, a Maya tribe who once settled in the area. With an area of only 5 sq km (3 sq miles), the city was never an urban metropolis on the scale of Cobá, Dzibilchaltún or Mayapán, rather a ceremonial and administrative capital.

The term 'Maya site' is something of a misnomer when applied to Chichén Itzá. True, there was a Maya city here, and it flourished during the Classic period, its structures making up the so-called **Central Group** (Old Chichén). However, the buildings that attract most visitors, those of the **Northern Group** (New Chichén) show a great deal of Toltec influence. After the decline and disintegration of the Maya civilization in the 10th century, a group of Toltec exiles conquered the city, rebuilding it in the image of their god Quetzalcoatl, or Kukulcán as he became known to the Maya. Kukulcán is usually depicted as a plumed serpent, and this sculpted image can be seen at the bases of the balustrades of the staircases surrounding the great Pyramid of Kukulcán. Another Toltec symbol seen throughout New Chichén is the peculiar reclining figure of Chac-Mool, thought to be a representation of fertility.

## KUKULCÁN PYRAMID

Despite the overthow of the Maya, elements of their religion and architecture were incorporated into the new order at Chichén Itzá. Nowhere is this more apparent than in the giant ★★★ **Kukulcán Pyramid** ❶, the site's dominant structure and the focal point of the city. The 24-meter (80-ft) high pyramid (dubbed simply El Castillo by the Spanish) is really a gigantic timepiece, a perfect representation of the Maya calendar, with four 91-step staircases plus a single step at the main entrance (or the one at the top, some say) adding up to 365. Eighteen terraces divide the nine levels which represent the eighteen 20-day months. The nine terraces symbolize the nine underground worlds. Each side has 52 panels representing the 52-year cosmic cycle, the point at which the two Maya calendars, the religious and the secular, coincided and then began anew.

## A STEEP CLIMB

The pyramid can be climbed via its western staircase. The climb is a steep one, made awkward

**Star Attraction**
● Kukulcán Pyramid

**The equinox**
At the spring equinox (21 March), thousands come to Chichén Itzá to witness a memorable event: the play of sunlight on the balustrade of the northern staircase gives the appearance of a living serpent that is creeping down toward the plumed serpent's head at the foot of the pyramid, to slither into the ground. This phenomenon was Kukulcán's signal that the time for sewing crops had arrived. In contrast, at the fall equinox (21 September), the snake appears to ascend, indicating that the crops should be harvested.

*The handrail is very useful for the descent*

Map below

by the narrow treads of the steps; on the descent, when it appears even steeper, you'll probably need to use the handrail in the middle. Note the sign at the bottom warning older visitors and those with respiratory problems of the dangers of the climb.

The flat-topped **temple** at the top of the pyramid is surrounded by a gangway which provides fine views of the entire site, including the Temple of the Warriors to the southeast. The carvings of warrior figures on the lintels of the temple evince clear Toltec influence. The main entrance leads to a narrow gallery that surrounds the inner sanctuary *(see below)*. A mask of Chac, god of rain and harvest, hangs over the entrance and there is reference to Kukulcán in the roof decoration, in the form of conch shells.

*The jaguar throne in the sanctuary*

## THE INNER SANCTUARY

Similar to other Maya pyramids, and in keeping with the custom of superimposing one monument over another at the end of a 52-year cycle, the Kukulcán Pyramid is built around an older structure. One of the highlights of the visit to Chichén Itzá is climbing up the steps of this building, now encased by the outer shell; access to the 61 steps is gained through a doorway at the side of the northern staircase (open only 11am–1pm and 4pm–5pm). At the top is the ★★ **inner sanctuary**, which is furnished with an altar or throne in the shape of a bright red jaguar with jade spots and eyes and real jaguar teeth; there's also a reclining Chac-Mool holding up a shallow sacrificial bowl, which would have held the heart of many a human victim. Caution: climbing the steps to the inner sanctuary is not for the claustrophobic.

**ROUTE 5 CHICHÉN-ITZÁ**
0      200m

Sacred Cenote ❺
Sacred Causeway

Temple of the Bearded Man
Ball Court ❼   Tzompantli ❻   Main Plaza   Platform of Venus
Platform of the Eagles ❹   Temple of the Warriors
Temple of the Jaguars   Kukulcán Pyramid (El Castillo)   ❷   Ball Court
The Counselor's House   ❶   ❸   Ball Court
Visitors' Center   Thousand Columns
The Ossuary ❽   Market   Steam Bath
Temple of the Deer ❾   Ball Court
La Casa Colorada   Xtoloc Cenote
❿   Observatory (El Caracol)
Steam Bath   Temple of the Carved Panels
Nunnery (Las Monjas)   Church   Akab-Dzib
❶❶   Annex
Chichén Viejo   Valladolid
Mérida

## TEMPLE OF THE WARRIORS

Evidence of Toltec residence at Chichén Itzá is most palpable at the ★★ **Temple of the Warriors ❷**, located across the plaza to the southeast of the Kukulcán Pyramid.

Named for the reliefs depicting thousands of Maya warriors, this structure bears a striking resemblance to a similar edifice at Tula, the old Toltec capital. Only four stories high, the larger platform at the top meant that a roomier temple could be built. In front of the temple is another reclining figure of Chac-Mool, its belly hollowed into a bowl to receive offerings. The feathered serpent pillars at the temple entance plus the interior columns may have been topped by wooden beams to support a roof.

Immediately to the south of the temple are the famous **Thousand Columns ❸**, stretching away into the jungle. Also once roofed over, this enormous colonnaded walkway, more reminiscent of the ruins of ancient Egypt or Greece than of Maya Yucatán, flanked what is thought to have been a **market**. Remains of steam baths and a number of ball courts are also in the vicinity; the baths were probably used as part of religious rituals, in order to prepare sacrificial victims or to perform cleansing rituals for high priests and rulers.

## SACRED CENOTE

From the Temple of the Warriors, skirt across the north side of the plaza , passing the **Platform of Venus ❹**, where sculptures depict the goddess as a feathered serpent devouring a human head.

**Star Attractions**
● **Pyramid inner sanctuary**
● **Temple of the Warriors**

*Below: among the Thousand Columns. Bottom: Temple of the Warriors, viewed from the Pyramid*

Map on page 62

Almost due north of the platform, the Sacred Causeway leads off between the trees. Now little more than a dirt track, this was once a paved highway to one of the most important religious sites in the city, the ★★ **Sacred Cenote ❺**. A huge limestone waterhole, measuring 60 meters (197ft) across and 21 meters (69ft) from rim to water level, this was not a place where the city's inhabitants came to slake their thirst, but where they ended up after being sacrificed. The grim truth about the Sacred Cenote came to the surface after explorations carried out in 1903–7 by US consul Edward Thompson. As well as precious ritual objects of jade and gold, he found human bones in the dark waters of the cenote. Hundreds more objects were salvaged by a second exploration under the direction of the National Geographic Society in the 1960s. The skeletons of men, women and children gave the cenote its other name, the Well of Sacrifice.

*Below: Platform of Venus*
*Bottom: Temple of Skulls*

## SACRIFICIAL OFFERINGS

Further reminders of the Maya penchant for human sacrifice are to be found back on the plaza, just to the west on the entrance to the Sacred Causeway. The ★ **Tzompantli ❻**, or Temple of Skulls, sports long rows of grinning skulls carved on the sides of its main platform. It is said that this is where victims of sacrifice had their heads

impaled on poles. The nearby **Platform of Eagles and Jaguars** has reliefs of eagles and jaguars holding human hearts, as well as symbols of Toltec warrior classes, one of whose duties was to capture 82 sacrificial victims.

**Star Attractions**
● **Sacred Cenote**
● **Ball Court**

## THE BALL COURT

Wind up your tour of the Toltec part of the city with a visit to the ★★ **Ball Court ⑦**, away to the left of the main entrance. A total of nine ball courts have been identified at Chichén Itzá, but with walls 82 meters (270ft) long and set 30 meters (98ft) apart, this is by far the biggest, and also the best preserved. As is the case with ball courts at other Maya sites, there is no sign of there having been any seating around the arena, indicating that the Maya Ball Game was not a mass spectator sport but perhaps some kind of exclusive ritual *(see box)*. The walls of the ball court are decorated with friezes showing players in protective clothing. They include a player holding a ritual knife in one hand and a decapitated head in the other; the headless body of the victim is depicted with writhing snakes, symbolizing blood, coming out of his neck. It might be assumed that these were the winning and losing captains respectively, though some say that it was the winners who were 'honored' in this way.

The selected few may have observed the proceedings from the top story of the so-called **Temple of Jaguars** on the eastern side, which would have acted as a kind of tribune. Access would have been up the side stairs.

**The Maya Ball Game**
The Maya Ball Game (Pok-Ta-Pok) involved two teams wearing lots of padding propelling a heavy latex ball around without using hands or feet, bouncing it off their hips and shoulders. The rings each side of the playing field, called the ball court, were a target for shooting the ball through – a seemingly difficult feat. The game is thought to have represented a battle between cosmic opposites: sun and moon, night and day, the life-giving gods versus those of the underworld. It has often been said that the losing team was sacrificed after these games, but some experts dispute this.

*The Temple of Jaguars*

## THE CENTRAL GROUP

The Central Group at Chichén Itzá, belonging to the original Classic Maya city, is situated in the trees to the southwest of the main plaza. It is well worth exploring the area: not only are there some fine buildings, but it's also much more peaceful away from the main plaza.

The first structure of any size, situated to the right of the track, is the **Ossuary ⑧**. Some 10

Map on page 62

*Below: the Red House*
*Bottom: the Observatory*

meters (33ft) tall, this pyramidal stucture contain crypts in which skeletons were discovered more than a century ago, together with jade and cerami offerings. Four staircases lead to the top, each dec orated with carvings of serpents.

The next group of buildings, again to the righ of the main track, includes the **Temple of the Deer 9**, a structure on a pyramidal base that onc had a fresco mural of deer-like figures. A little further on is the **Red House**, so named by the Spanish for its once red door, but known by the Maya as Chichan-chob (House of Small Holes for its lattice-work; it is a Puuc-style platform with rounded corners and has a mask of Chac, the rain god, on the roof comb. Climb to the top for a good view of this part of the site.

## THE OBSERVATORY

A little further on, to the left of the track, is one of the finest buildings on the entire site, the ★★ **Observatory 10**, also called the Caraco (snail) because of its winding interior stairway The building, which is elevated on two platforms is a perfect example of celestial alignment. It wa constructed over a period of several centuries being modified and added to as new discover ies in astronomy were made. The remarkable thing about it is its resemblance to modern-day

observatories, the main difference being that there were no telescopes but slits in the roof through which certain stars appeared at particular times. Astronomer-priests would use their studies of the heavens to plan festivals, rituals and harvests, and to predict the exact times of the equinoxes. Beside the Observatory is the **Temple of Sculpted Panels**; the most interesting feature of this structure is the relief work depicting figures of warriors, trees, and animals.

**Star Attractions**
● **Observatory**
● **Nunnery Church**

## THE NUNNERY

The last group of structures, reached up some crumbling steps at the far southern boundary of the site, is the so-called **Templo de las Monjas** (the Nunnery) ⓫, a partly collapsed palace complex 35 meters (115ft) wide, 65 meters (213ft) long and 20 meters (66ft) high, which proably housed Maya royalty but was named by the Spanish for its resemblance to a convent. With their intricate decoration and moldings, the buildings are a fine example of classic Maya architecture in the Puuc style of Uxmal, Kabáh and Sayil *(see pages 84–8)*. Of particular note is the so-called Annex, festooned with masks of Chac, including the ones built into corners of the structure.

The free-standing building off to the side is known as the ★★ **Church**. One of the oldest buildings on the site, and the most richly carved, it pays homage to the *bacah*, a group of four gods said to have held up the sky. The panel of masks depicts the four *bacabs* in their natural forms of armadillo, rabbit, turtle, and snail.

## THE MUSEUM

The site museum provides some written information on the city of Chichén Itzá and displays some artefacts. The visitor complex in which it is housed is also a good place to rest in air-conditioned comfort if the heat and sun become too much for you, and also to pass the time while waiting for the Sound and Light show to begin. There is also a cafeteria and a restaurant.

**Writing on the wall**
A short walk to the east, behind the Nunnery, is the Akab Dzib. The name means 'Temple of Obscure Writing', after the Maya glyphs that fill the dark interior. As you enter, you might get the impression that the walls are 'talking' to you, but you don't know what they're saying. That's because you don't read ancient Maya hieroglyphics, but the Maya believed that only those pure in spirit could read the inscriptions on these walls.

*Entrance detail at the Nunnery Annex*

Map on page 69

**A name lives on**
Mérida was founded in 1542 on the site of the ancient Maya city of T'ho. Maya speakers continue to refer to the city by its old name.

*Below: Mérida Cathedral*
*Bottom: Governor's Palace*

# 6: Mérida

The elegant city of Mérida, the capital of the state of Yucatán, combines the tradition and culture of old-world Spain with the fast-paced growth of modern-day Mexico. Mérida has expanded enormously in recent years into a bustling city of some 1 million inhabitants, but this in no way detracts from the appeal of the place. The historic core remains defiantly intact, and Mérida is a relaxing and pleasant place to stay as well as being an ideal base from which to explore the Yucatán.

## EUROPEAN INFLUENCE

Mérida has an unmistakably European feel. Since the first colonists arrived in the mid-16th century, the city has been shaped by a steady stream of European adventurers, influencing not only its architecture but also its fashion and education. And because of its isolation from the rest of Mexico, it was to Europe that Mérida always turned for ideas and inspiration. The city's greatest period of prosperity came with the henequen boom of the 19th century. The henequen barons lavished their wealth on Mérida, and the mansions they built made the city a veritable showcase of neoclassical architecture, particularly along the grand Paseo de Montejo.

The city was laid out on a symmetrical grid pattern, and surrounded by a wall with a grand arch at every exit point. Nothing remains of the wall today, though three of the original 13 arches still stand. Each of the large grids created its own *barrio* (neighborhood), complete with its own amenities and church, but the focal point of Mérida was always the central **Plaza Grande**, and this is where our tour begins.

## CITY TOUR

The plaza, with its pleasantly shaded central park, is surrounded by fine buildings. On the north side is the ★**Governor's Palace** ❶ (open daily 8am–10pm). Built in 1892, the palace has an airy arcaded courtyard, where on the first floor you can admire a series of bold murals by Fernando Castro Pacheco. Begun in the 1950s and finished almost 25 years later, they depict events in the history of the Yucatán from Maya times to the post-colonial era. Near the entrance on the ground floor is a **tourist information office**, which has maps and leaflets with information on the huge variety of cultural events that the city has to offer (*see box on page 71*).

## THE CATHEDRAL

On the northeast corner of the Plaza, rising above everything else, is ★★**San Ildefonso Cathedral** ❷ (open daily 6am–7pm). The cathedral, with its striking twin towers, was built between 1561 and 1598, making it one of the oldest in the Americas. The conquistadors had the cathedral constructed with the stones taken from the dismantled temples of the original Maya city of T'ho, as if to symbolize the arrival, and triumph, of Christianity over indigenous religious rituals and beliefs. Mexican rebellions (such as the War of the Castes) and the revolution of the early 20th century stripped the cathedral of its original treasures – all apart from a sculpture

**Star Attraction**
● San Ildefonso Cathedral

*Detail of a Pacheco mural in the Governor's Palace*

Map on page 69

*Below: Casa de Montejo courtyard*
*Bottom: Teatro Mérida*

known as **Cristo de las Ampollas** (Christ of the Blisters). Supposedly carved from a tree that burned unharmed all night, after being struck by lightening in the villlage of Ichmul, it is revered by Meridians, who hold an annual festival in its honor from 28 September to 13 October. The huge 20-meter (66-ft) wooden Christ above the altar was a gift from Spain.

Beside the cathedral is an open **Galleria** that would not look out of place in Florence or Rome. The space is used by the city for temporary exhibitions of sculpture. It is flanked on the south side by the **Museo Macay ❸** (Museum of Contemporary Art, open Wed–Sun 10am–5pm), which has an extensive permanent collection of work by local and national artists, as well as temporary exhibitions.

On the south side of the plaza is the ★★ **Casa de Montejo ❹**, built in 1549 by Francisco de Montejo, Mérida's founding father. Today, the building houses a bank, Banamex, but it is possible to walk through the entrance to admire the lush courtyard. The intricately carved facade includes busts of family as well as carvings of armed warriors standing on the heads of the vanquished Maya. Maya heads also support the heavy pediments over the windows and entrance.

On the west side of the plaza is the **Ayuntamiento ❺** (City Hall, open daily 10am–10pm), with its arcaded facade and slender clocktower. It's worth a peek inside to see some modern murals, one depicting the threat of nuclear war.

## AWAY FROM THE SQUARE

When exploring the rest of Mérida it is important to remember that even street numbers run north-south, odd numbers east-west. From the City Hall, head a short distance north up Calle 62 for a look at the facade of the ★ **Teatro Mérida**. Fully restored in the late 1990s and housing a cinema and piano bar, it is a fine art deco building.

Also worth seeing to the west of the Plaza Grande is the **Casa de las Artesanias** (Calle 63 No 503 between Calles 64 and 66). Housed in the restored convent of Monjas, it has a selection of local arts and crafts. To the east of the Plaza, behind the cathedral on Calle 61, is the ★ **Museo de la Ciudad** (open Tues–Fri 10am–2pm and 4–8pm, Sat & Sun 10am–2pm). It is housed in the former church of San Juan de Dios and features drawings, maps, plans and photographs relating to the planning and growth of Mérida. Further east, at the corner of calle 50 and 59 in the former Monasterio la Mejorada, is the **Museo de Arte Popular**, which has a small collection of costumes and handicrafts from all over Mexico.

## ALONG CALLE 60

Heading north away from the Plaza Mayor, along Calle 60, you will pass **Parque Hidalgo**, dominated by the Jesuit-built church, **La Tercera Orden**; this church built in 1618, contains a painting which depicts the meeting in 1546 of Montejo and Tutul Xiú, the Maya ruler, who became a convert to Christianity, thus inducing most other local chiefs to follow his lead.

A little further along, opposite the Universidad de Yucatán, is the domed **Teatro Peon Contreras** (built in 1900), whose ornate marble staircase was designed by the Italian architect Enrico Deserti, also responsible for the city's Anthropological Museum. In the little park in front (Plaza de la

**Star Attraction**
● Casa de Montejo

**A happening city**
Mérida and culture go hand in hand. An extensive program of events, held every night of the week, includes *ballet folklórico*, concerts of different types of music from pre-Hispanic to modern jazz, theater productions, and events for children. Proceedings usually start at 9pm; there may be a small charge.

Then every Sunday, the Plaza Grande and surrounding streets are closed to traffic to make way for the fiesta called *Mérida en Domingo*, with music of all kinds, folk dancing, children's events. At 7pm, in front of City Hall, a large band plays latino music and locals and visitors dance, carouse, and generally have a great time.

*Plaza de la Maternidad, along Calle 60*

Map on pages 69 & 76

**Ticket to ride**
Much of Mérida can be seen on foot, but getting to the Paseo de Montejo or the Anthropology Museum is the perfect excuse to take a ride in a *calesa*, or a horse-drawn carriage. Other vehicular transport is provided by the old-fashioned tour bus, the Transportadora Turística Carnaval, which leaves the Parque de Santa Lucía four times daily (10am, 1pm, 4pm, 7pm), and takes in 30 sights on its two-hour itinerary.

*Elegant villa on the Paseo de Montejo*

Maternidad) is the **Monumento de la Madre** with a statue of a mother and child.

When you get to the **Parque Santa Lucía**, take a look at the ★ **Poet's Corner** with its array of busts commemorating Yucatán's cultural and artistic history, including Cirilo Baquiero, father of Yucatecan song. The park is the setting for the Sunday outdoor *artesanía* market, as well as music or dance events on Thursday evenings.

## PASEO DE MONTEJO

Continue on Calle 60 to **Parque Santa Ana**, turn right, and two blocks further on begins the ★★ **Paseo de Montejo ❻**. Fashioned after the Champs Elysées in Paris, this shady boulevard is where the tycoons of the henequen industry, who earned their fortune by exploiting Indian laborers on their plantations, erected their grand mansions. Some of them still stand today, and it's not hard to imagine the lives of elegant luxury that were led behind their walls. The ornate **Palacío Cantón** (Calle 43 and Paseo de Montejo) now houses the ★★ **Museo de Antropología e Historia** (open Tues–Sat 8am–8pm; Sun 8am–2pm). Alongside its fine collection of Maya artefacts, the museum seeks to explain the complex facets of Maya society, including trade patterns and social customs; on the first floor, displays relate the methods used to excavate various sites.

Further along the Paseo is the **Monumento a la Patria** (National Monument). The circular construction was designed by Romulo Rozo in 1946. The central lake and fountain represent both the local aquatic wildlife and the city of Tenochtitlán (present day Mexico City), where the Aztecs built their capital. The images carved into the gray stone (brought from the town of Ticul) relate the history of Mexico, from the time of the Maya to the Spanish conquest. Each of Mexico's 32 states are represented here with their coats of arms.

In addition to monuments, Mérida has a number of parks, including the pleasant **Parque de las Americas**. Another creation of Romulo Rozo, it is located on Calle 21.

## EXCURSIONS

Around 22km (14 miles) to the north of Mérida, just off the main Highway 261 to Progreso, are the ruins of ★★ **Dzibilchaltún** (open daily 8am–5pm). Dzibilchaltún, meaning 'where there is writing on stones', was an important religious and commercial center, continually occupied from as early as 500BC until the Spanish conquest.

With an economy based largely on salt, it is thought to have had a population of some 20,000 at its height (AD600–900). Much of the 13 sq-km (5 sq-mile) site has been left to the jungle, but several hundred structures have been unearthed, including the enormous ★ **Palace** at the southern side of the central plaza. Near the palace is the open-air **Xlacah Cenote**, exploration of which has yielded thousands of Maya sacrificial offerings, including human skeltons, but which centuries ago became a watering hole for livestock. It is now a good place for a swim.

**Star Attractions**
- **Paseo de Montejo**
- **Anthropology Museum**
- **Dzibilchaltún**

*Below: climbing the palace steps at Dzibilchaltún*
*Bottom: the Dolls' House*

## THE DOLLS' HOUSE

The most intriguing structure at Dzibilchaltún is the **Templo de las Siete Muñecas** (the Temple of the Seven Dolls), named after the seven small clay dolls that were found here. Each doll had a bodily deformity, but it is not clear whether they were simply a child's toy, or whether they

Map
on page
76

*Below: the lighthouse
at Progreso
Bottom: Progreso beach*

had any religious significance. What certainly is significant is the temple's alignment, whereby its four openings frame the segments of the sky marked by the soltices and the equinoxes. At these times of the year, direct sunlight 'pierces' the building, and a specialist is usually on hand to explain the phenomenon.

The seven dolls are now housed in the ★ **Museo del Pueblo Maya** near the entrance, well worth a visit for its insights into ancient and colonial culture. Pride of place is occupied by a plumed serpent from Chichén Itzá.

## PROGRESO

★ **Progreso** is the closest beach town to Mérida, 35km (22 miles) north of the city at the end of Highway 261. *Progreso* is Spanish for 'progress' but this once charming colonial town has no great pretensions of being, or even ever becoming, a tourism mecca. This is where the locals go on holiday, and it is predominantly locals, including weekenders from Mérida, who frequent the lively beachfront restaurants or go picnicking on the unremarkable beach, which is flanked by the shipping wharf, Puerto de Altura (a lengthy concrete pier to compensate for the shallow sea) and a lighthouse. However, if rumoured vehicle ferries from Tampa and Houston materialize, the town'

town's tourist economy should rack up a few notches. Certainly gringos have already begun to colonize the coast to the east, in a string of resorts known locally as **La Costa Esmeralda**.

The first are some classy places near to the little fishing village of Chicxulub. After that, you'll spot signs all along the coast for beachside holiday complexes, but it's best to wait for the seaside village of **Telchac**, with its beach cabañas at the casual Casa del Mar or the elegant Reef Club, if you want more comfort. Beyond lie Chabihau and finally **Dzilam de Bravo** where the road ends. From here you can rent boats to take you to the Boca de Dzilam lagoon in the **Parque Natural de San Felipe**, a great place for wildlife watching.

## CELESTÚN

Easily accessible from Mérida on the west coast is a wildlife sanctuary famous for its flamingos. Take 281 for 92km (57 miles) to the fishing port of **Celestún**, perched on a narrow peninsula connected to the mainland by a causeway across the lagoon. The lagoon is part of a national park, the **★★ Parque Natural del Flamenco Mexicano de Celestún**, where, as at Río Lagartos (see pages 54–5), flamingos, herons and other wildlife are under official protection.

Tourism is more organized here than at Río Lagartos, the hub of operations being the purpose-built **Cultur** visitors' center, with its naturalist exhibits, snack bar, and boat dock for excursions. The flat-bottomed boats are operated by experienced skippers who have taken to tourism after the decline of the local fishing industry. The standard 2-hour excursion explores the mangrove-ringed lagoon, offering possible sightings of flamingos, as well as turtles, crocodiles, pelicans, egrets and sometimes spider monkeys. You'll also visit the Tampeten pertified forest and, at the southern end of the lagoon, the Real de Salinas, where salt is still extracted and shipped out.

Longer trips for dedicated birdwatchers can be arranged through Cultur.

**Flamingos**
Flamingos, males and females identical in size and appearance, form monogamous couples, and live as long as 30 years or even more. They obtain food by filtering plankton through the sensitive hairs on their tongue. Flamingos are resident at Celestún (and Río Lagartos) all year round, but their numbers swell considerably during the northern winter when thay are joined by migrants from the Mississippi Delta and elsewhere.

*Flamingos at Celestún*

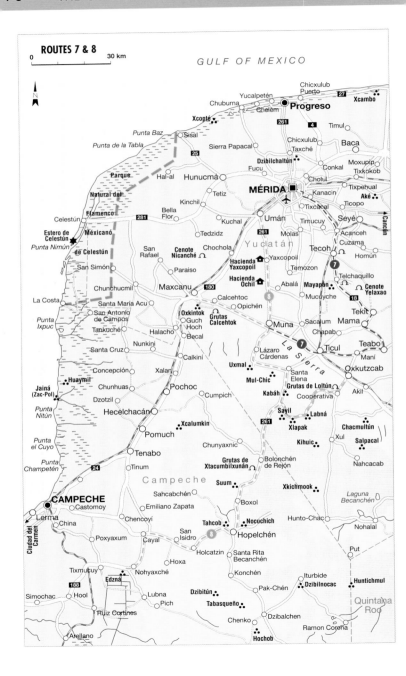

## ROUTES 7 & 8

0 — 30 km

GULF OF MEXICO

# 7: The Convent Route

**Mérida – Acanceh – Tecoh – Telchaquillo – Mayapán – Mama – Teabo – Maní – Ticul – Muna – Mérida (120km/79 miles)**

This route involves a journey out into the countryside to the south of Mérida, taking in a series of towns and villages where vestiges of the Maya and colonial cultures exist side by side. At the time of the conquest, this region belonged to the Xiu Maya, the first native allies of the Spanish and the first converts of the Franciscans traveling with them. The order invested heavily in the region and it remained a Franciscan stronghold throughout the colonial period. The settlements lie on what is commonly referred to as the 'Convent Route'. It takes you to within reach of the great Maya city of Uxmal on the 'Puuc Route', described in the next chapter.

## ACANCEH

From Mérida, follow Highway 18 to the south. Recently upgraded, the road now bypasses most of the towns. After 31km (19 miles), you will reach the turn-off for ★★ **Acanceh**, a lively little market town famous for its Plaza de las Tres Culturas, where pre-Hispanic, colonial and modern-day structures lie cheek by jowl. Dominating the square is the church of **Nuestra Señora de la Natividad**. A fine example of Franciscan style architecture, it was built using the stones of pre-Hispanic buildings. Opposite, and adjacent to the grocer's, baker's and other modern buildings, is the **Pyramid**. Measuring 32 meters (105ft) on each of its four sides and 15 meters (49ft) tall, this is just one relic of ancient Acanceh which reached its height during the Early Classic period (AD300–600); the most intriguing thing about it are the enormous ★ **masks** that were unearthed from its flanks in the late 1990s. Another Maya structure is the nearby **Palace of Stuccos**, which sports a stucco-decorated frieze, superimposed with figures of monkeys, bats and other animals related to the Maya underworld. There are also

Map opposite

**Star Attraction**
● Acanceh

*Below: the church and (bottom) the Maya pyramid at Acanceh*

Map on page 76

*Below: the Pyramid at Mayapán*
*Bottom: at the market in Tecoh*

features reminiscent of the Teotihuacan style, suggesting that Acanceh was a Teotihuacan enclave.

Continue along Highway 18 to **Tecoh**, 50km (31 miles) southeast of Mérida, where a former convent, the **Virgin of the Ascension**, is based upon what may have been a Maya pyramid. Also of interest is the local cenote, whose cavern has some wonderful stalactite and stalagmite formations and is ideal for a cool swim.

Just south of Tecoh, it's worth stopping at the small town of **Telchaquillo** for a look at the Franciscan temple, whose carved facade – worked by Maya artisans – has representations of Chac (the god of rain) and several animal figures. In the center of town there is a staircase leading to a cenote with some good examples of stalactites. If you didn't see the caves at Tecoh, then a stop at this cenote is a must.

## MAYAPAN

Just beyond Telchaquillo is the ancient Maya stronghold of ★**Mayapán** (open daily 8am–5pm). This sprawling city, which is estimated to have had 12,000 inhabitants at its height, but which is now mostly lost to the jungle, was together with Uxmal and Chichén Itzá, part of the powerful Triple Alliance, a confederation that ruled most of the Yucatán between AD987–1185.

The alliance ended when the Mayapán leader, a Toltec named Hunac Ceel, took sole control. His dynasty continued to rule the region for 200 years until, in 1441, according to the *Chilam Balam* – the Maya 'Bible' – the city was almost completely destroyed by invaders from Uxmal. A century later, Mayapán was one of the last cities to fall to the Spanish.

More than 3,500 structures have been identified at Mayapán, of which over 100 are thought to have had a ceremonial function. The site is being increasingly opened up to visitors, with an ongoing program of excavation and restoration, and it's interesting to see how the structures are transformed from jungle-covered mound to recognisable building. One of the centerpieces is the ★ **Kukulcán Pyramid**. It is the same design as the one in Chichén Itzá *(see page 61)*, though on a much smaller scale.

## TO MANÍ

The route continues south through an area riddled with cenotes, past Tekit, and then on to **Mama**, with its impressive Franciscan monastery, which was built in the 16th century but subsequently expanded. From Mama, turn left along a minor road to **Teabo**, another town where a Franciscan convent was planted right on top of a Maya pyramid. It is possible to sleep in the convent, and similar hospitality awaits in nearby ★ **Maní**, which was capital of the Xíu Maya and one of the most important Maya centers in the 16th century. Maní, whose sorrowful name in Maya means 'the place where everything has stopped', was the scene of the infamous burning of the books by Bishop Landa *(see box)*. The church and convent of **San Miguel Arcángel**, at which Landa carried out his deed, dates from 1548. In the chapel inside are a series of reliefs depicting the battles fought by the conquistadors for the territory, and a stone depicts the legend of an early Maya chief, Tutul Xíu. There is also a restaurant in the town bearing his name; serving excellent Yucatecan food, it draws visitors from all over Mexico.

---

### Burning the books

Maní was the scene of one of the saddest episodes in the history of the Yucatán. It was here, in July 1562, that Bishop Diego de Landa gathered together hundreds of 'idols' and all he could find of the Maya scriptures and publicly burned them in front of the Church of San Miguel Arcángel, thereby destroying virtually all Maya recorded history and at the same time easing their conversion to Christianity. Ironically, Landa was fascinated by Maya culture and civilization, and his book *Before and After the Conquest* remains the most reliable account we have of Maya history.

*Church of San Miguel Arcángel at Maní*

Map on page 76

**Culinary legacy**
The popular Yucatecan dish *poc chuc* (pork fillet with onion and spices) is claimed to have been invented in Ticul at the **Los Almendros** restaurant. There are now branches in Cancún and Mérida, where you can try it at lunchtime.

*Pottery is a prominent industry in Ticul*

## TICUL

The busy town of ★ **Ticul** sits at the junction of Highway 18 and Highway 184, 86km (53 miles) from Mérida. As you pass through, you can't fail to notice the clay sculptures that mark every square and crossroads. On account of its location in one of the very few areas of the Yucatán where clay can be found, the town has become famous for its red ceramics. Pottery stores can be found all over, but most of the workshops are on Calle 23. They include **Arte Y Decoración Maya** (Calle 23 between 38 and 40), which turns out excellent copies of stelae, Jaína masks, glyphs, and many other pieces of pre-Hispanic art. As the number of shoe stores testifies, the town is also known for its footwear, which is designed and made locally, and exported widely.

At the center of town is the convent and church of **San Antonio**. A Franciscan mission was established here in 1555; by 1591 it had attained the rank of *cabecera*, or head mission, and construction on the great church and convent began. The mark of the Franciscans is seen throughout the church, with symbols of the order and knotted cord embellishments around the doorways.

## MUNA

About 22km (14 miles) to the northwest of Ticul, along Highway 184, is **Muna**, the main access point for Uxmal on the Puuc Route *(see page 84)*. The town concentrates almost exclusively on the production of *huipil* embroidered dresses and other clothes, and locals sell their products from shady huts in a square just off the main road.

Opposite is the **Chun Yaax Che** restaurant (Trunk of the Sacred Ceiba Tree), well known for its excellent Yucatecan cuisine. Here, too, at their Los Ceibos workshop in front of the restaurant Patricia and Rodrigo Martin Morales make and sell their fine replicas of ancient Maya vases, masks and other items.

From Muna, you can either continue your journey to Uxmal and other Puuc sites, or head back to Mérida along Highway 261 *(see opposite)*.

# 7: The Puuc Route

**Mérida – Yaxcopoil – Manu (– Oxkintok) – Uxmal (– Kabáh – Sayil – Xlapak – Labná – Grutas de Loltún) – Grutas de Xtacumbilxunán – Edzná – Campeche (322km/229 miles)**

There are two routes from Mérida to the port city of Campeche, one which follows a direct line along highways 180 and 24, and the other which takes the long way round , south to Muna and then across the Puuc Hills to Hopelchén before striking west. The latter leads to some amazing Maya sites, all representative of the distinctive Puuc style *(see page 84)*. Plan on spending a couple of days touring the area; if you want to break up the route, the sites around Kabáh can be seen as a day trip from Mérida, as can Edzná and the spots around Hopelchén as day trips from Campeche.

## MORE HACIENDAS

Head out of Mérida on the Highway 180 as if going to Campeche, but at Uman bear south along the 261. At km 33, you'll pass the small village of Yaxcopoil, dominated on the right-hand side of the road by the enormous **★★ Hacienda Yaxcopoil** (open Mon–Sat 8am–6pm, Sun 9am–1pm). Yaxcopoil ('the place of the green poplars' – *Alamos Verdes*) dates from the 17th century, and

Map on page 76

**Star Attraction**
● Hacienda Yaxcopoil

*Below: henequen at Ochil*
*Bottom: palace facade at Sayil*

Map on page 76

*Below: Hacienda Yaxcopoil*
*Bottom: water-lily at*
*Hacienda Ochil*

at its height, during the boom years of sisal cultivation in the late 19th and early 20th centuries, the estate here covered some 9,000 hectares (22,000) acres. Today, it is the Yucatán's principal hacienda museum.

The buildings are well preserved, but not overly restored. It's as if time has stood still at Yaxcopoil. The main building, entered through a triple archway, consists of two parallel ranges. In the left-hand range, with its high ceilings, is the office, the living room, reception room, bedrooms, bathroom and chapel, all with original period furnishings. Pride of place in the living room is taken by oil paintings of Don Donaciano García Rejón and his wife Doña Mónica Galera, who acquired the hacienda in 1864. The other range houses the kitchen and dining room, as well as the Maya Room, where pieces of pottery and other finds from the small ruins scattered around the estate are on display. It's also possible to visit the factory complete with machinery. Opposite the main building is a Maya village, its inhabitants descendants of the Maya who once worked on the estate.

## HACIENDA OCHIL

Continue south on the 261. After about 7km (4 miles), there is the turn-off to **Hacienda Temozón**, which as been restored and converted into a luxury hotel. Just after this turn-off, on the right-hand side of the road, a nice place to break the journey is ★ **Hacienda Ochil**. This hacienda has also been restored, and in the main house there is a museum with relics from its functioning past. The old chapel now houses a good crafts store, selling some of the items produced in the on-site **workshops**. The shady butler's house, situated above the hacienda's very own cenote, is now a pleasant bar, while typical Yucatecan dishes are served at the patio restaurant at the main house.

## OXKINTOK

Continue to Muna *(see page 80)*, the gateway to the Puuc hills and its Maya treasures. However, ou may first want to make a detour back to the uuc site of ★ **Oxkintok** (open daily 8am–5pm), ocated just south of the junction of Highways 180 nd 184 (the most direct way of getting here from 1érida is straight down the 180).

Oxkintok was a major power in the Puuc region uring the Classic period. There are several groups f buildings, but the most famous structure is the '**zat Tun Tzat**, which has numerous rooms con-ected by doors and passageways and steps. The te is also known for the hieroglyphic inscriptions n some of its monuments and stelae, which show ome of the oldest Long Count dates yet found for ucatán. Notable, too, are the **warrior statues** that ppear to be guarding Ch'ich Palace. Perhaps the 1ost interesting feature of Oxkintok, however, ; the **labyrinth**. Apparently unique in the entire ucatán, it is thought to be connected to the main yramid by a tunnel.

Nearby are the ★ **Grutas Calcehtok** (also alled Grutas Xpukil), one of the largest cave sys-ems in the Yucatán. Much of the sytem is still ) be explored, but numerous Maya relics and rtefacts have been found here, and the caves were sed as a refuge during the War of the Castes. The aves are unlit, so you need to go with a local uide. The most interesting one, Number 4, has atural formations called 'the crocodile', 'the orse', 'the tongue' and 'the divine face'.

**Stage set**
As you enter Yaxcopoil, you have the feeling of walking onto a gigantic stage set; indeed, many Mexican and Hollywood west-ern movies have been filmed here.

*The Tzat Tun Tzat at Oxkintok*

Map
on pages
76 & 85

### The Puuc style

Much of the form and detailing of the buildings at Uxmal is pure Puuc style, recognizable by its sophisticated architecture of clean lines, rounded walls, ornate stone frescoes, intricate lattice-work, rows of columns and high vaulted arches. Many Puuc buildings are flat, low and elongated, built on artificial platforms and laid out in quadrangles. They are perhaps the most elegant ruins in the Maya world.

## UXMAL

From Muna *(see page 80)*, Highway 261 winds its way up into the Puuc hills, after 2km (1½ miles) reaching a high point with superb views in every direction. Gone is the monotonously flat northern Yucatán, ahead lie gently-rounded hills swathed in thick jungle. After 16km (10 miles) you find the entrance to ★★★ **Uxmal** (open daily 8am–5pm), by far the largest of the Puuc sites, and after Chichén Itzá, the most visited Maya city in the Yucatán. The name Uxmal means 'three times built', implying the city was inhabited on more than one occasion and the structures were not all built at the same time.

## PYRAMID OF THE MAGICIAN

Entering the site, the most impressive structure is the ★★★ **Pyramid of the Magician**, which derives its name from the legend of it having been built in one night by a child magician borne of a sorceress. In reality, the structure (which is really five structures, one on top of another) took almost three centuries to build. The pyramid is distinctive for its rounded contours; according to one story they were created so that Ehécatl, the god of the wind, would not hurt himself on any sharp edges when he blew over the structure. The climb to the top is very steep and difficult – despite the

*Pyramid of the Magician, Uxmal*

ain handrail. The temple on the upper platform
covered with Venus symbols. The views of the
te and surrounding jungle are magnificent from
re, but if you don't feel like the climb there
e plenty of other vantage points on the site.

## NUNNERY QUADRANGLE

 the north of the pyramid is the ★★ **Nunnery
uadrangle**, so named by Father Diego López
 Cogolludo, who was reminded of a Spanish
nvent when he visited the site at the beginning
 the 17th century. The entire complex is built
 an elevated man-made platform. The Quad-
ngle has a total of over 70 rooms along its four
nges, and may have been used as ancient mili-
ry barracks or some other form of residence;
ere's a rumor that sacrificial victims spent their
st few months here in debauchery. Each range
orts its own distinctive décor. Chac masks dom-
ate the north range, Venus symbols cover the
nge to the east, the southern range has several
rvings of *na*, thatched huts, and the west range
ows signs of Toltec influence with carvings of
uetzacoatl, the feathered serpent.

## HOUSE OF TURTLES

eave the quandrangle through the archway on the
outhern side, go down the steps and then
ead south across the lawned main plaza,
assing the remains of a small **ball court**.
 little further on is the delightful ★ **House
f the Turtles**. The design of this build-
g, its setting (overlooking the main plaza)
nd the unique turtle-motif ornamentation
ave led many to proclaim it to be one of
e finest in the Maya world. The turtle was
ssociated with the rain god, Chac, so it is
nderstandable that there is a building dec-
rated with turtle images in this water-bar-
en region. The turtles are near the top and
re depicted as if walking horizontally on
e wall. The upper third of the walls are
rnamented with mosaic panels.

**Star Attractions**
● Uxmal's Pyramid of
the Magician
● Nunnery Quadrangle

*Corbelled arch at the
Nunnery Quandrangle*

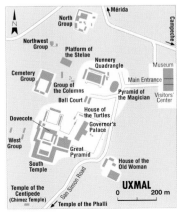

Map
on pages
85 & 76

**Light show**
The Visitors' Center at the entrance to the ruins includes a store, museum and a restaurant that stays open until 10pm. This is handy for visitors who want to stay on for the ★★ **Sound and Light Show** (English-language version at 9pm). The Uxmal show is considered to be even better than the one at Chichén Itzá.

*Steps of the Great Pyramid, with the Governor's Palace*

## GOVERNOR'S PALACE

Behind and to the left of the House of the Turtles is the ★★ **Governor's Palace**. All of 100 meters (330ft) long, this enormous structure is a masterpiece of Puuc architecture. The Puuc style of building was to face rubble-filled walls with cement and cover the whole with limestone mosaic panels, in this case no less than 20,000 of them. These and other details – corbelled arches, intricate doorways and delicate carvings – can be viewed at close quarters, from the terrace that surrounds the building.

## THE GREAT PYRAMID

A short walk through the jungle behind the palace will bring you to the **House of the Old Woman**. The witch who lived here was supposedly the mother of the dwarf magician who built the Magician's Pyramid. Returning to the plaza, beside the palace is the ★ **Great Pyramid**. This is a copy of the one at Chichén Itzá, though on a much smaller and less detailed scale. It has been well restored, however, and you can climb to the top for stunning views of the whole site, the Governor's Palace in the right foreground and the Magician's Pyramid looming in the distance.

The **South Temple** complex has not yet been restored and is difficult to explore because of the thick vegetation. The last structure of interest is the **Dovecote**, so named by the Spanish because of the latticed roof-combs. It is likely the structure was used for astronomical study.

## KABÁH

Continue south on the 261, through the small village of Santa Elena, to arrive at ★★ **Kabáh** (open daily 8am–5pm), the first of a quartet of smaller Puuc sites. Kabáh ('Mighty Hand') straddles the highway and consists of three groups of buildings, of which the most interesting is the East Group, comprising two large structures thought to have had administrative functions. The dominant one is the rectangular **Palace** that rises majestically above the main grassy plaza and contains about 30 rooms, but equally important is the **Codz Poop** ('rolled straw mat'), whose west facade is festooned with hundreds of grinning Chac masks.

The Central Group includes a pyramid and the freestanding, but rather crudely restored, **Arch of Kabáh**, which marked the start of what was once a *sacbe* (elevated road) to Uxmal and another one to nearby Labná *(see page 88)*.

## SAYIL

A short distance beyond Kabáh is a turning on the left signed 'Ruta Puuc'. Follow this minor road to visit the other sites in the quintet, starting with ★★ **Sayil** (open daily 8am–5pm). Sayil, which means 'place of the leaf-cutter ants' in Maya, is highly recommended, not just for its architecture, but also for its location, set amongst a cluster of low, jungle-covered hills. The most impressive structure by far is the three-story **Great Palace**, whose imposing south-facing facade is stepped back in terraces. It contains almost 100 rooms which would have been used for a variety of functions, such as storage, government offices and residences. The second story is punctuated with short columns, the lintel above adorned with reliefs of the gods, including the upside down Descending

**Star Attractions**
● **Governor's Palace at Uxmal**
● **Sound and Light Show**
● **Kabáh**
● **Sayil**

*Below: a Chac mask*
*Bottom: Kabáh's Palace*

Map on page 76

**Wealthy area**
The Maya settlements of the Puuc region were very rich in Classical times because of the fertile soil. The region produced, and in fact still produces, several crops a year, where farmers in the rest of the peninsula could only manage one or two. The surpluses allowed the communities to support artisans such as stonemasons, who created such wonders as the arch at Labná and the palaces at Kabáh and Sayil.

God, as also seen at Tulum *(see page 42)*. O the grassy plaza in front of the palace, there ar eight visible *chultunes* (stone cisterns), which th Maya used for saving rainwater during the lon dry season. It's worth taking a walk along the pa through the trees at the other side of the plaza t see **El Mirador**, a squat temple on a pyramida base surmounted by an enormous roof comb – th latter more typical of the Peten region Guatemala than anywhere in the Yucatán.

## XLAPAK AND LABNÁ

Next up is **Xlapak** (open daily 8am–5pm), minor site but one whose small Palace, with it intricate workmanship, is considered one of th jewels of the Puuc style.

The last of the Puuc sites in this area is ★ Labn (open daily 8am–5pm). There are many similari ties between the structures at Labná ('Abandone House') and those at Sayil, the most obvious exam ple being the **Great Palace**, which, like Sayil, prob ably had three stories originally, though only tw now remain. But the site is best known for th ★ **Arch**, or Great Gate, which forms the entrance t the main palace group (at the opposite side of th site to today's entrance). The arch itself is 5 meter (16ft) high and 3 meters (10ft) wide, and is a typ ical example of a false Maya arch, i.e. a corbelle

*The Arch of Labná, a lithograph by Frederick Catherwood*

arch with no keystone. It is flanked on either side by small rooms thought to have been guardhouses, and the whole structure is decorated with classic Puuc-style features, including niches in the form of Maya huts *(na)* over the entrances to the guardhouses – similar to those on the south range of the Nunnery Quadrangle at Uxmal *(see page 85)*.

## GRUTAS DE LOLTÚN

A little further along the same road, shortly before the junction with Highway 184 at Oxkutzcab, are the ★★**Grutas de Loltún** (open daily 9am–5pm; guided tours taking about an hour in English and Spanish). A visit to Loltún, which means 'the place where the rock became flowers', is a must, not just for the caves' astonishing natural rock formations, but also for their human history, which has provided archeologists with a unique window on the pre-Maya and Maya world. Bones of the long extinct mammoth and bison have been discovered here, as have prehistoric stone tools, but the most striking man-made features are the pottery, petroglyphs and paintings left by the Maya. The petroglyphs include the delicate floral motifs that gave the caves their name, and among the paintings are 'negative' images of hands, created by blowing soot over a real hand placed against the cavern wall.

The interconnecting caverns are about 1km (⅔ mile) long and some chambers reach a height of 45 meters (150ft). Near the entrance is a bas-relief known as the **Warrior of Loltún**, dating from the late Pre-Classic period and evincing definite Olmec traits. In addition to the Maya artworks, you can admire the various limestone formations with evocative names such as 'Cathedral' and 'Grand Canyon Gallery'.

Of special interest are the 'musical' columns, formed by the union of stalactites and stalagmites, that produce sounds with different tones when they are knocked; there is also a gallery whose ceiling has collapsed to allow in descending tree roots and daylight. At various points, *chaltunes* (cisterns) have been carved out of the rock for collecting drip water.

**Star Attraction**
● **Grutas de Loltún**

*Below: inside the Loltún caves*
*Bottom: ancient hand prints*

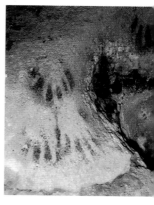

Map on page 76

**Hidden woman**

The legend of the caves says that Timot, tyrannical ruler of nearby Bolonchén, banished his daughter Lolbé to the caves on hearing of her forbidden love affair with a peasant, Dzulín (the name Xtacumbilxunán means 'hidden woman'). Dzulín was determined to find his true love, Lolbé, and with the aid of a magic potion, entered the caves, where the young couple spent the rest of their lives hiding together. There is a small tribute to the star-crossed lovers in the caves.

*Temple of the Five Stories at Edzná*

## GRUTAS DE XTACUMBILXUNÁN

From the Loltún Caves, you can either continue to Oxkutzcab and link up with the Convent Route *(see page 77)*, or double back to Highway 261 and head south toward Campeche. Shortly after the small town of Balonchén de Rejón, there is a sign on the right to the ★ **Grutas de Xtacumbilxunán**. These caves were 'discovered' in 1841 by John Lloyd Stephens and Frederick Catherwood *(see page 15)*, and one of Catherwood's most famous lithographs is that of the colossal wooden ladder leading down into the cave, with a dozen Maya carrying water jugs. Today, an old local woman will take you into the giant cavern, using a handheld torch for illumination. However, you need a good imagination to see the 'snake, dog, eagle' limestone shapes that are advertized.

## EDZNÁ

At Cayal, 42km (26 miles) beyond Hopelchén, turn south for a further 18km (11 miles) to reach **Edzná** (open daily 8am–5pm). Standing at the center of an extensive system of irrigation canals, and located on a major Maya trading route, this Pre-Classic city was already thriving by AD100. It continued to prosper for another 800 years, until abandoned around AD900.

The main reason for any visit here is to see the imposing ★★★ **Temple of the Five Stories**, a stepped palace pyramid almost 30 meters (100ft) high, by the main plaza. From the base, a central staircase (65 steps) rises through five levels to a three-roomed temple. On May 3 (and August 8) the sun alights on a stela in the center of the temple, marking the start of the Maya agricultural year. Each door is illuminated directly by the sun on a different date once a year.

Arranged around this central area are various lesser buildings, including the **Temple of Masks**, lined with stuccoed masks representing the Sun God, and the **Great Tribune**, an amphitheater with seating for up to 5,000 people who would come to watch the ceremonies and sacrifices conducted on the central platform in the square.

# 8: Campeche

Walking the flagstoned streets of old Campeche, the first-time visitor is struck by what a stunningly colorful place it is. Almost the entire Old City has been restored to its original splendor, its squat ★★ **colonial mansions**, with their spacious courtyards, painted in a whole variety of bold hues: pinks, greens, blues, yellows and browns. And surrounding this sea of color are the restored remnants of the city wall, the bulwark towers (*baluartes*) that once guarded against attack from both land and sea. The combined effect is striking, and in 1999 UNESCO declared this historic city a World Heritage Site.

Map on page 92

**Star Attractions**
● Edzná's Temple
● Campeche's mansions

*Below: along Campeche's ramparts*
*Bottom: colonial mansions*

## WEALTH AND PIRACY

The leisurely atmosphere of Campeche today belies its often turbulent past, a past largely dictated by its situation, right on the Gulf of Mexico. It was founded in 1540 by Francisco de Montejo the Younger, on the site of a Maya trading village called *Ah Kim Pech*, but only after fierce resistance from the locals that had seen off an expeditionary force under Francisco Hernandez de Córdoba in 1517. The town soon became the peninsula's gateway for shipping, from where galleons laden with cargos of gold and silver, as

**Map below**

**Trolley bus**
Visitors who prefer to ride rather than walk can take a tour round the Circuito Baluartes aboard the Tranvía de la Ciudad, a trolley bus. It runs 4 times each day from the Parque Principal, and the tour lasts around 45 minutes.

well as precious woods, set sail for Spain. With all this concentration of wealth, Campeche became the target of pirates who launched their raids from headquarters established at Ciudad del Carmen further down the coast. Their names are like a who's who of buccaneering, including such figures as John Hawkins, Henry Morgan and Francis Drake, to mention just the British contingent. The worst assault came in 1663, when the buccaneers of several nations joined forces in an onslaught of unprecedented ferocity, raping the women, slaughtering the populace and destroying many of the buildings. The Spanish had had enough, and set about encircling the city with a 3.5-meter (11-ft) thick wall, creating one of the few fortress cities in the Americas, a hexagonal stronghold guarded by eight towers. The pirates were forced to redirect their energies elsewhere.

After Mexico's independence in 1821, Campeche became a provincial backwater, with an economy based on fishing. However, its walls saved it again during the War of the Castes, when Maya insurgents had taken every town in the peninsula except Campeche and Mérida. Campeche is still an important fishing center today, though much of its recent prosperity has come from oil.

## CITY TOUR

Most of the city's sights are located on or within the Circuito Baluartes, the road marking the line of the old city walls, most of which were dismantled at the end of the 19th century when the *Campechenos* decided they no longer needed such protection from attack.

Begin the tour at the ★ **Parque Principal ❶** at the southern edge of the Old City. The small shady park in the middle, with its attractive pavilion, is a popular place for locals to come and relax with a newspaper, or get their shoes shined. At the southern side of the square is the **Casa Seis**, which preserves the interior of a 19th-century house with original furnishings,

### Map labels

Gulf of Mexico

Avenida Ruiz Cortínes

Reducto de San Miguel ❽

Congreso del Estado

Av. 16 de Septiembre

Puerta de Mar ❶ ❷ Casa Seis

Parque Principal

Catedral de la Concepción

Mansión Carvajal

Plaza del 4 Centenario

Baluarte de Santiago Jardín Botánico ❼

Av. Circuito Baluartes Norte

Baluarte de San Pedro

Baluarte de San Carlos ❹

Museo Regional de Campeche

Baluarte de San Francisco

Baluarte de Santa Rosa

Puerta de Tierra ❺

Av. Circuito Baluartes

Baluarte de San Juan

Mercado ❻

Alameda

Costa Rica

Av. República

**ROUTE 9 CAMPECHE**

0    200 m

Baluartes Sur

Pedro Moreno

Av. Central

nd has an attractive inner courtyard. There is also tourist information desk here.

The square is dominated on its north side by the mposing ★ **Catedral de la Concepción ❷**. Dating from 1540, it is the oldest church on the peninula, though its baroque twin towers are from a ater date. Two blocks along Calle 10 from the athedral is the **Mansión Carvajal**. This enormous two-story mansion belonged to a wealthy acienda owner, Don Fernando Carvajal Estrada. t now houses a local government office, but it s still possible to go inside and admire the striking black and white checked floors, the sweeping taircase and the Moorish arches of the covered ourtyard, features which attest to the considerble wealth that once flowed through the city.

## ΜAYA STELAE

Closing the square on the west side is the newly restored **Public Library**, whose arcades mirror hose of the Portales del Centro opposite. To the eft of and behind the libary is the **Baluarte de a Solidad**, one of the eight defensive towers ringng the city, together with a short stretch of the ïity wall. Today it houses the ★ **Museo de Estelas Mayas**, which includes an impressive collection of Maya stelae taken from a number of sites, including Edzná. The figures and

*Below: Catedral de la Concepción*
*Bottom: Museo de Estelas Mayas*

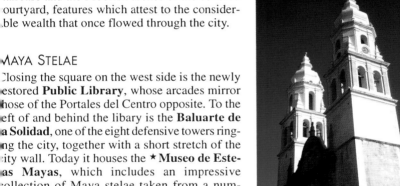

Map on page 92

**Botanical oasis**

Some of Campeche's *baluartes* have not been used as creatively as they might have been. One very notable exception is the **Baluarte de Santiago ❼** at the northwest corner of the Old City, which contains a tiny but very lush ★★ **Botanical Garden**. With its shady palms and a variety of other immaculately tended exotic trees and plants, and a pathway that snakes among them, this is a really pleasant place to relax and cool off.

*Tropical oasis in the Baluarte de Santiago*

hieroglyphs on the stelae are explained in Spanish. Adjacent is the **Puerta del Mar ❸** (Sea Gate), which was rebuilt in the 1950s when its value as a tourist attraction was realized.

## TOUR OF THE BULWARK TOWERS

From the Sea Gate, follow Calle 8 past the imposing Palacio Municipal on the left, and a group of modern buildings on the right – including the flying-saucer like **Congreso del Estado** – to arrive at the sturdy **Baluarte de San Carlos ❹**. It houses the city museum, worth a visit to see the maps, photos and an architectural model of the city as it was when the walls were intact. A ramp leads up to the roof, a good point from which to survey the city. The huge domed building to the east was the Church of San José, but is now a cultural center.

From San Carlos, you can continue to walk around the Circuito Baluartes, but it is much more pleasant to cut back to the Sea Gate and take a stroll along Calle 59 to the **Puerta de Tierra** (Land Gate) ❺, at the opposite side of town. A room inside houses a small collection of armaments including muskets and cannonballs, and for a small fee you can go up onto the roof, where there are several cannons pointing away from the city. The only substantial remaining stretch of the **city wall** connects the Land Gate with the **Baluarte de San Juan**, and it's possible to walk along the parapet, though the only way down is to return to the Land Gate. Adjacent to the Land Gate is the **Baluarte de San Francisco**, which contains offices and is not open to the public, though you can go up the ramp onto the roof.

Due east, at the other side of the Circuito Baluartes, is a shady park, **Alameda Francisco da Paulo Toro**, which has a series of *paseos*, or walks, originally intended for the elite to parade in their carriages. The adjacent **Mercado ❻** is a fascinating place to observe the daily life of the poorer residents of the city, a warren of dimly lit aisles, and stalls piled high with all manner of products. Further round to the north, pass the **Baluarte de San Pedro** before returning to the starting point.

## REDUCTO DE SAN MIGUEL

Three kilometers (2 miles) south of the city center, on Buenavista Hill, stands the largest of all Campeche's fortifications, the 18th-century **★★ Reducto de San Miguel 8** (open daily 9am–7pm). With its snaking entranceway, drawbridge and battlements, the fort is considered a first-class piece of military engineering. Recently renovated, it is now home to the **Museo de Arqueología Maya**, a new museum displaying an impressive variety of Maya relics and artefacts from sites in Campeche, arranged in the nine rooms surrounding the central courtyard.

Highlights include clay figurines from the nearby island of Jainá. These realistic statuettes were buried with the dead, and have played an important role in determining how the ancient Maya lived and what they wore. There are also jade masks and a host of other objects from the great Maya city of Calakmul *(see page 98),* as well as numerous stelae, fragments of friezes and statues of the gods. With its state-of-the-art interactive displays, the museum is probably the best on the entire peninsula, the only potential drawback for English-speaking visitors being that all the explanations are in Spanish.

From the battlements, where the old cannon are still in place, the views of the city and the Bay of Campeche are magnificent.

**Star Attractions**
- **Botanical Garden**
- **Reducto de San Miguel**

*Below: hardware on wheels*
*Bottom: Reducto de San Miguel*

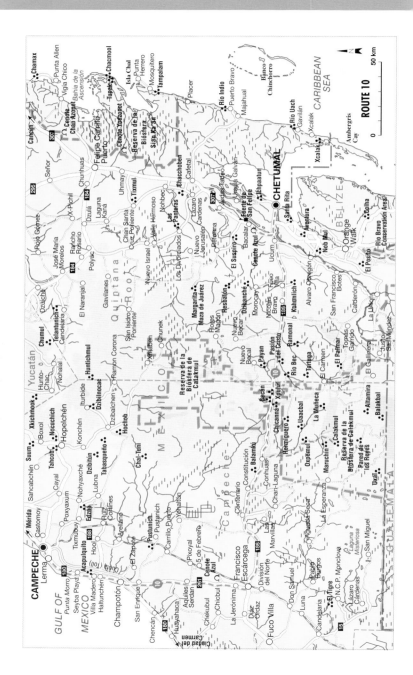

# 9: Campeche to Chetumal

**Campeche – Escárcega – Balamkú – Calakmul – Chicanná – Becán – Xpuhil – Kohunlich – Chetumal (351km/219 miles)**

Swathed in thick jungle, the southern Yucatán is the least accessible part of the peninsula. But it is also one of the most rewarding to visit, for hidden in the jungle is the largest concentration of ruins anywhere in the Maya world. Some of the sites, including the great city of Calakmul, are located within the vast **Calakmul Biosphere Reserve**, the second largest protected area in Mexico, whose tropical rainforest is home to an astonishing variety of animal and birdlife *(see page 11)*.

Starting in Campeche, follow either the coastal Highway 180 or the toll motorway along the shore of the Bay of Campeche to **Champotón**. There are a few shabby local resorts along this stretch of coast, but not much to entice the visitor. From Champotón, head inland to **Escárcega**, a major junction for traffic heading along Highway 186 east to Chetumal and west to Chiapas. The next settlement of any size going east, Xpuhil, is 152km (95 miles) away, so if you intend to visit the ruins of Calakmul *(see next page)*, it's wise to stock up on provisions here.

## BALAMKU

Head east along the 186. After 52km (32 miles), there is an oasis of sorts in the shape of the **Laguna Silvituc**, where the restaurant/bar 'La Laguna' serves meals and refreshments under its palapas at the lake shore. At km 93 (58 miles from Escárcega), a turning on the left leads to the first of a series of Maya sites just off the highway.

Rediscovered in 1991, **Balamkú** (open daily 8am–5pm), which means 'Jaguar Temple', is visited primarily for the unique stucco ★ **frieze** found under one of the pyramids in the central group of structures. Dating from between AD550–650, and measuring 17 meters (56ft) by 4 meters (13ft), the two-story frieze is richly embellished with

Map opposite

Map opposite

**Battle site**

Champotón marks the site of the Spaniards' first landing on Mexican soil (after their brief landing on Isla Mujeres) under Francisco Hernández de Córdoba, on 20 March 1517. But the landing was not a happy one: the local Maya went on the offensive, inflicting heavy losses on their adversaries. Córdoba died soon afterwards, in Cuba, from the 33 wounds he had received in the battle.

*Ruins in the jungle, Calakmul*

Map on page 96

**Stelae**
A feature of Calakmul are the numerous carved stelae, more than 100 in all, dotted around the site. Many depict luxuriantly attired personages, probably local rulers, standing on top of prisoners. They also have calendar glyphs that show dates between AD514 and AD850, corresponding to Calakmul's main period of greatness.

*Structure I at Calakmul, the tallest pyramid in the Maya world*

carvings of giant masks of Itzamná, the Earth Monster, crowned by regal-looking, mythical animals. There are jaguars too, as well as crocodiles and toads, and from the mouths of the masks ferocious serpents burst forth. The whole composition represents the Maya perception of their world above ground and the underworld beneath.

## CALAKMUL

Eight kilometers (5 miles) further on, at km101, you'll arrive at the hamlet of **Conhuas**, from where a black-top road on the right leads into the heart of the Calakmul Biosphere Reserve and the great Maya ruins of Calakmul. A toll is charged at the junction, and it takes about an hour to drive the 60km (38 miles) along the road to the site. The reserve itself is open from 6am–7pm, but because the site closes at 5pm it is advisable to get here good and early (you may prefer to start out from Xpuhil).

There isn't much to distract you on the road to the ruins, except the endless rainforest and the occasional family of ocellated turkeys crossing the road in front of you. When you finally arrive, there's a pleasant walk of about 1km from the car park to the ruins themselves.

### CITY OF TWO ADJACENT PYRAMIDS

★★★ **Calakmul** (open daily 8am–5pm) is a place of superlatives. The immense site, covering an area of 67 sq km (26 sq miles), is the largest known city of the Maya world, comprising over 6,500 structures, including the largest Maya pyramid ever found. The first surveys of the site took place in the 1930s. However, because of its isolation, it was to be more than 40 years before archeologists began to wrest Calakmul from the jungle.

Calakmul, whose name means 'City of Two Adjacent Pyramids', reached its height during the late Pre-Classic and Classic eras. With an estimated population of 50,000, this was a superstate of the Maya world, vying for control of the Maya lowlands with its great rival, Tikal. The site is famous for the elaborate tombs that were discovered here, together with a series of magnificent jade funerary masks, examples of which can be seen at the Reducto de San Miguel in Campeche *(see page 95)*.

**Star Attraction**
● Calakmul

## HIGHLIGHTS

Most of Calakmul's restored structures are grouped around the jungle-shaded **Central Plaza**. Crossing the Plaza, you'll pass between two low buildings, a group of three temples (structure IV) on the left and an observation platform (structure VI) on the right. Together they formed an **astronomical complex**, the temples marking the positions of the rising sun at the summer solstice (north temple), the winter solstice (south temple), and the equinox (central temple).

There are a number of stelae near the complex *(see box)*, and more to be found at the base of Structure II, which dominates the end of the Plaza. This massive **pyramid** is the second-largest structure on the site. Imposing now, it must have been a truly awesome building in its heyday, for much of its facade would have been adorned with giant stucco masks. As you climb up the central stairway, you'll pass a series of platforms and terraces on either side, and a couple of tunnels that disappear into the bowels of the building. The top of

*Below: detail of stelae near the base of Structure II on the Central Plaza (bottom)*

Map on page 96

**Río Béc style**
The sites around Xpuhil are all examples of the Río Béc style. The style is characterized by buildings of well cut stone blocks covered with stucco, their corners rounded, with high towers and often temples embedded in the major structures. Such structures tend to be covered in deep relief carvings, with steep steps leading to small, enclosed rooms.

*The three towers of Xpuhil*

the main structure is crowned by rooms of a palace dating from the late Classic era, and beyond this a secondary pyramidal complex extends even higher. It is only when you get to the very top that the ★★★ **views** really open out. In every direction, the rainforest of the Calakmul Biosphere Reserve stretches toward the horizon.

Far away to the south, across the border in Guatemala, you may just be able to make out the pyramids of the great city of Tikal peeping above the canopy. Much closer, to the southeast, you'll see the other Calakmul pyramid (Structure I) rising out of the jungle. Still being restored, this is the tallest pyramid in the Maya world, rising an awesome 50 meters (164ft) from the jungle floor.

## XPUHIL

Further east along the 186, at km 152, is the busy little town of **Xpuhil**, a good place from which to explore some smaller but nonetheless very interesting sites in the vicinity, which have all been loosely termed Río Bec *(see box)*. Xpuhil has a few budget hotels, of varying quality, if you want to spend the night in the area. There are a couple of restaurants and a mini-supermarket for food supplies. There are usually a few taxi drivers parked up beside the highway waiting for tourists to arrive. If you want they will spend the day with you, acting as chauffeur and tour guide of the nearby sites.

The most accessible of these sites, Xpuhil, Chicanná and Bécan are just off Highway 186. ★ **Xpuhil** lies just at the western edge of town, and visitors should definitely take along some mosquito repellent for the walk through the jungle to the site. Xpuhil means 'Place of the Cat Tails' in Maya, and it was named by members of the fourth Carnegie Expedition to Campeche, who 'discovered' the site in 1938. It's most interesting feature is **Structure I**, which essentially consists of three towers (or very steep pyramids), built as a monument to local artistic prowess rather than for any particular function. Some of the decorative motifs still exist, but in their heyday the towers would have had intricately decorated roof combs, and the frieze of the base structure would have been festooned with masks of Itzamná.

Itzamná, the God of Creation or 'Earth Monster', features even more strongly at the next site, ★ **Chicanná** ('House of the Snake's Jaws'), located 5km (3 miles) west of Xpuhil, just to the south of the highway. Here, take a look at Structure II in particular, where the gaping mouth of the god, complete with a fearsome set of teeth, actually forms the entrance. Still intimidating today, the power this entrance to the underworld exerted over local Maya priests would have been incredible.

## BECÁN

The sculptural decoration at Chicanná gives an idea of what the less well preserved facades at nearby ★★ **Becán** might have looked like. Judging by its size, and by the fact that it was surrounded by a defensive moat, Bécan was probably the local capital of these sites, which reached their heyday between AD550 and AD800. Discovered in 1934, Bécan has long been a good place to explore, but its gleaming, newly-restored **Pyramid**, which is visible from the main road, makes it doubly worthy of a visit. The pyramid is by far the the tallest structure on the site and is situated on the **Central Plaza**, which is reached

**Star Attractions**
● **Calakmul views**
● **Becán**

*Below: decoration on Structure X at Becán Bottom: a view of the site from the pyramid*

**Map on page 96**

*Below: trees and ruins at Kohunlich*
*Bottom: stucco mask of Chac in the Temple of the Masks*

along a discreet, vaulted passageway. A climb to the top is well worth the effort for the view of the surroundings and the site itself. The two other main buildings around the Central Plaza are **Structure VIII** in the east, with its superstructure of twin towers on a pyramidal base, and **Structure X** in the west, where in addition to sculptural decoration there are still some limestone mosaics to be admired. Beyond is the small ball court.

The other main plaza is the **Southeastern Plaza**, an interesting combination of platforms, pyramids and monumental buildings, some used for residential purposes. It's fun to explore here, particularly the interior of **Structure IV** with its passages and stairways.

## KOHUNLICH AND DZIBANCHÉ

Some 58km (36 miles) east of Xpuhil, a narrow road on the right leads after 9km (6 miles) to the Early Classic city of **Kohunlich**. Set around expansive plazas and amid groves of palm trees, this is one of the most attractive sites on the peninsula. Devoid of any vast structures, it is most famous for its ★★ **Temple of the Masks**, an Early Classic pyramid whose central stairway is flanked by huge stucco masks representing the rain god, Chac. Built around AD500, this temple is one of the oldest structures at the site; it was subsequently covered over with a Terminal Classic construction, which accounts for the marvelous state of the masks' preservation today.

To the north of Highway 286, reached via the village of Morocoy, is another site that is well worth a visit, ★★ **Dzibanché**. The imposing ruins here feature massive pyramid temples, whose roof combs make them typical not of any other style in the Yucatán, but of the Peten style associated with Guatemala; indeed some archeologists have dubbed Dzibanché 'the Tikal of Mexico'. The site, which flourished during the Classic period from AD300–800, gets its name 'Writing in Wood' from the wooden lintel found at the top of the huge Temple VI near the entrance, bearing glyphs corresponding to the date AD618.

## CHETUMAL

The capital of the state of Quintana Roo, Chetumal is situated on a vast bay, just north of the Belize border at the end of Highway 186. Goods have been shipped from Chetumal since ancient times, when the Maya conducted a thriving export trade in cacao. Today's exports are mostly hardwoods from nearby forests.

The modern appearance of Chetumal is due to its reconstruction after disastrous hurricanes in 1942 and 1955. Things to see in the city are somewhat limited, but the ★★ **Museo de las Culturas Mayas** *(see box)* is well worth a visit. To the north of the city, the Bulavar Bahía winds attractively along the seafront to the palm-fringed village of **Calderitas**, with its minor Maya site.

## BACALAR

Some 38km (24 miles) from Chetumal, going north on Highway 307, is the town of Bacalar. This is a popular place on account of the **Laguna de Siete Colores**, whose turquoise waters are perfect for fishing and boating. Overlooking the lagoon, near the Balneario de Bacalar (swimming area in the lagoon) is the **Fuerte de San Felipe**, built in 1729 as protection from pirate raids. Just south of the town is the **Cenote Azul**, one of the largest cenotes on the peninsula.

**Star Attractions**
- Kohunlich
- Dzibanché
- Maya Museum

**Maya Museum**
Whether you've already visited the sites or not, the **Museum of Maya Culture** in Chetumal provides an excellent introduction to the civilization's way of life, history and achievements. From the crops grown by Maya farmers to the different kinds of Maya arch to the Maya method of counting, it's all here among the numerous hands-on displays. And if you want to familiarize yourself with city layouts, just look at the miniature reconstructions under the glass floor.

*Dusk at the Laguna de Siete Colores*

# The Ancient Maya

In addition to the Yucatán, the Maya people settled almost all of what are today's Guatemala and Belize and parts of Honduras and El Salvador. Often referred to today as the Mundo Maya, their territory covered an area of more than 300,000 sq km (116,000 sq miles). There were different Maya groups, sometimes allied with each other and sometimes fighting, but they all shared common beliefs, social structures, languages and an architecture that clearly define them.

The Maya civilization developed from small farming communities to larger settlements built on local trade to great cities that held sway over entire regions. Its success was based on a highly sophisticated system of farming and irrigation, the principal crops being maize, squash, beans, and tobacco. Surplus production led to trade, and trade created a strictly hierarchical society.

Much of what we know about the Maya today is the result of primary research carried out by the Spanish at the time of the conquest, though it was also the Spanish who burned many of the Maya codexes and idols, believing them to be the work of the devil *(see page 79)*. Other information, notably the dates and other details of rulers, has been gleaned from cracking the code of the Maya glyphs carved onto walls and stelae.

## SCIENCE AND RELIGION

By the time of its cultural flowering between AD300–AD900, the so-called Classic period, the Maya had developed a highly advanced civilization, not only in terms of art and architecture, but also science and technology. The Maya created the concept of zero and invented their own system of numerals, based on a dot for the numbers one to four, a bar for the number five and so on. The only writing system native to the Americas was invented by the Maya; it involved the use of over 800 individual glyphs or symbols, which represented words, syllables or images. The observation of the heavens and the calculation

**Maya calendars**

Over the centuries, the Maya developed two different but inter-related calendar systems. The Maya Round Calendar consisted of 20 named days which interlocked like a cogwheel with the numbers one to 13, giving a total cycle of 260 days. Alongside this system was one more closely based on the sun's movement, with 18 months each 20 days long and a further five days at the end to complete the solar cycle of 365 days. These two calendar systems came back to their starting point every 18,980 days, or 52 years, signifying a rebirth. Interestingly, every 52 years was the frequency with which the Maya added a new layer to their temple-pyramids.

*Above: Detail from a surviving codex*
*Opposite: Chichén Itzá*

### Maya gods
The Maya had 166 named deities. The gods took on many different forms, often depicted as being either male or female, young or old; and they had a different appearance at night, as they entered the underworld. Ixchel, usually depicted as a female figure, was the goddess of fertility, medicine, childbirth, weaving and the moon. Chac was the god of rain, harvest, cenotes, lightning, tobacco, and the cardinal points. The comical-looking Descending God, depicted upside down with legs like a frog, is thought to have been the god of honey. Some groups believed in a supreme being, Itzamná, the god of Creation. Masks of the gods – Itzamná and Chac in particular – commonly feature as decorative motifs on Maya buildings, together with depictions of rulers and beasts.

*Stone mask of Itzamná in the Nunnery Quadrangle, Uxmal*

of time based on the movement of the stars was vital to the Maya. Many great cities, such as Chichén Itzá, had observatories from where the experts could calculate the calendar. The planet Venus was particularly closely monitored as it was linked with success in war, its appearance prompting the decision to attack. Venus was so important that it had the status of a god.

The Maya were deeply religious and repaid the gods for their existence by showing fidelity to them and providing the rituals they demanded, including blood sacrifice. They carved representations of their gods on temples and stelae. The rulers were spokesmen for the gods; they would wear the symbols of the heavens, typically the sky belt of the moon, the sun and Venus, day and night; and also dress in jaguar skins (the spots representing stars). Royal headdresses were representative of individual gods and were often made with quetzal feathers, jade, shells and flint. The precious jade was even inlaid in the rulers' teeth.

The Maya conceived of the world as flat and square, and among their most important gods were the four *Bacab* who occupied each corner. They were each identified with a color (white for north, yellow for south, red for east and black for west), and between them held up the heavens where the other gods lived. There were thirteen layers in the Maya heaven, each identified with a particular god; it is thought that the Maya gods had their doubles in the underworld, where, like the sun, all gods had to pass to be reborn.

## ARCHITECTURE

Many buildings would have been constructed from wood and thatch, long rotted away, so what remains are the elaborate administrative and ceremonial structures, including temples to the gods and rulers, palaces, ball courts and observatories. Ceremonial buildings were precisely aligned with the points of the compass and special attention was given to equinox and solstice settings. The most striking examples of these gigantic timepieces are the Pyramid of Kukulcán at Chiché

tzá *(see page 61)* and the Temple of the Seven
Dolls at Dzibilchaltún *(see page 73).*

Maya architecture is characterized by a sophisticated sense of decoration and art, expressed in
as-relief carvings and wall paintings. Styles dif-
ered by region and influence. In the Yucatán they
include the Classic Puuc style of Uxmal *(see page
74)* and the decorative Río Béc style of the south
*(see page 100),* but there are also influences from
the neighboring Peten region of Guatemala, particularly in the great cities of Calakmul *(see page
8)* and Dzibanché *(see page 102).* After the
decline of the Classic Maya civilization in the
10th century, thought to have been brought about
by civil wars between the different dynasties,
the hub of Maya culture became concentrated in
the northern lowlands of the Yucatán. Outside
influences came to bear, most notably those provided by the Toltecs at Chichén Itzá. War and
uncertainty necessitated the construction of defensive ramparts, such as existed at Mayapán, the last
of the major Maya centers *(see page 78),* or at the
coastal stronghold of Tulum *(see page 41).*

*Below: Temple of the Deer
at Chichén Itzá
Bottom: traditional
Maya dwelling*

## Colonial Architecture

During the colonial period, the country was
rebuilt in the image of Spain. Churches had top
priority and were built over Maya temples, often

*Below: Maya rug with the distinctive diamond pattern*
*Bottom: replica of a Maya figurine from the island of Jaína*

using the very same stone. In the Yucatán it wasn't just the main cities of Valladolid and Mérida that received this treament, but smaller settlements as well, such as Izamal *(see page 56)* and the towns and villages stretched out along what is now called the Convent Route *(see page 77)*. Mérida, Valladolid and Campeche are the most conspicuously colonial of the early cities. Mérida is additionally well endowed thanks to the henequen boom in the second half of the 19th century *(see page 16)*. The 'henequen barons' lavished their wealth on Mérida, making it a showcase of neo-classical architecture.

## Vernacular Design

While the ancient cities are in ruins, living Maya villages remain throughout the Yucatán. The traditional houses *(na)* are built according to the same basic design as ancient Maya dwellings, featuring walls of either mud, wood or stone with rounded corners, thatched roofs and dirt floors.

Today, the rural Maya continue to work small plots of land and to produce, in tandem with their town-dwelling counterparts, everyday practical items that make up a wide range of handicrafts. Basketware is made from sisal and other plant species found in the area, as are woven mats. Weaving was always important to the Maya, with fabric produced on personal looms incorporating traditional patterns and colors, and used for blankets and rugs as well as items of clothing. Important motifs include the diamond and the cross, both of which represent the four corners of the Maya world (in many modern Maya villages, the cross contains protective powers and is placed at crossroads or at sacred areas of the natural landscape). Terracotta pots have been a basic cooking utensil for generations of Maya families, and in places like Ticul *(see page 80)*, skills have been adapted to produce all manner of replica Maya artefacts. The finely woven hammocks, sold in all tourist centers, are indigenous to the Maya world, as are the traditional *huipil* embroidered dresses worn by Maya women.

# Festivals

**January 6** Día de los Santos Reyes. The Three Kings visit children and bring gifts of toys. Families celebrate Epiphany with a special wreath-shaped bread with a baby Jesus doll baked inside.

**March 21** Spring Equinox. This was an important day for the ancient Maya. Thousands of people gather each year to witness a spectacular natural light show at Chichén Itzá *(see page 61)*.

**March/April** Semana Santa. Holy Week is celebrated in grand style, with reenactments of the events of Easter taking place in most towns. Mock crucifixions are held on Good Friday, and Judas figures are burned on Saturday. (The Judases are papier mâché figures of popular 'bad guys', filled with fireworks, which are literally 'blown up'.)

**November 30–December 8** Descent of the Virgin. Festival celebrated on Isla Mujeres in honor of the local 'virgin'. Another large festival at Izamal in honor of the Virgin of Izamal.

Every town has its festival, often involving rodeos and bullfighting. One of the most spectacular is the Xímatkuil Fair held at a restored hacienda near Mérida during the first week of November.

### Honoring the dead

On November 1–2 is Día de los Muertos. Every part of Mexico celebrates this tradition of honoring the dead. In the Yucatán, mestizo Maya groups mix ancient rituals with modern day tradition. Some groups in the state of Campeche bury the bones of their loved ones in ornate boxes. On this day, they unearth the boxes and 'clean' the bones. While the 'Day of the Dead' traditions might seem morbid, they are anything but; they are a happy celebration of times past.

*Dancing on the Plaza Grande, Mérida*

# FOOD AND DRINK

Mexican cuisine is a rich blend of the indigenous Aztec and Maya culinary traditions and the Spanish and Middle-Eastern influences introduced by the conquistadors. Much has evolved since the Spaniards first arrived, and the Yucatán in particular, because of its location, has been subject to European influences. But the staples of the cuisine are essentially the same as they were in pre-Hispanic times, namely corn, beans and chilies.

## ESSENTIAL INGREDIENTS

Corn is used primarily for making tortillas, which are served either as an accompaniment to, or as an integral part of, many meals. *Tacos* are tortillas rolled or folded around a filling of shredded barbecue pork, beef or chicken, plus vegetables, either eaten as they are or grilled or fried. *Enchiladas* are stuffed tortillas smothered in sauce and baked. *Tostadas* are crisp, fried tortillas, that come with a variety of toppings. *Tostaditas* (otherwise known as 'tortilla chips') are tortillas cut in segments, deep-fried and usually served as a starter with salsa and/or guacamole. *Quesadillas* are tortillas stuffed with cheese and fried, and often served with refried beans.

Beans usually come in the form of *frijoles refritos* (refried beans), which are served as an accompaniment to many Mexican dishes, just as vegetables may be served in the West.

Chili peppers have been cultivated in Mexico since prehistoric times. There are many varieties, including the large, red ancho, with a rich, mild flavor, and the green, tapered serrano, which is hotter, and the jalapeño which is hotter still. Hottest of all, however, is the habañero, which commonly accompanies Yucatecan food.

## EGGS, MEAT AND FISH

Mexicans do interesting things with eggs. A breakfast favorite is *huevos a la Mexicana*, eggs scrambled with a mix of onion, tomato and chili peppers. *Huevos rancheros* are fried eggs on a bed of tortilla and refried beans with a tomato and chili sauce. Eggs also come scrambled with spicy sausage (*chorizo*).

As far as meat is concerned, the people of the Yucatán have traditionally eaten chicken, turkey and pork, but today you can find beef on the menu, especially steak. Surrounded as it is by water, the Yucatán has always had seafood in abundance, and visitors should not pass up the opportunity of trying some. A very popular fish dish is *pescado a la Veracruzana*, Veracruz-style fish – traditionally red snapper (*huachinango*), or grouper (*mero*), topped by a fragrant sauce of tomatoes, onions, capers and olives, scented with cinnamon. Fish in all varieties are served grilled, broiled or breaded. Conch (an abalone-like shellfish), shrimp and whitefish, marinated in lime juice, then seasoned with

**Yucatecan cuisine**
Any dish described as 'a la Yucateca' will have ingredients marinated or cooked in *achiote*, the ground seeds of the local annato tree mixed into a paste of cumin seeds, garlic, peppercorns and sour-orange juice. There are a number of local specialties which are prepared in this way, notably *poc chuc* (thinly cut pork) and *pollo* or *cochinita pibil* (chicken or pork baked in banana leaves – traditionally, though no longer very commonly, in earth ovens). All over the Yucatán you'll also find the refreshing *sopa de lima* (chicken soup with tortilla flavored with lime juice).

> ☀ **Juices and *licuados***
> Probably the most tempting drinks the Yucatán has to offer are its fresh-fruit juices, including orange, mango, melon, papaya, grapefruit and pineapple. A variation for the non-citrus fruits are the *licuados* (milk shakes), with mango, pineapple and banana being the most popular. Juices and *licuados* are available at most restaurants, but there are also juice bars. For a truly mouthwatering choice, try Janitzio on Mérida's Plaza Grande, which also specializes in fresh fruit ices and sorbets.

tomato, onion, chili and coriander, are components of the popular appetizer called *ceviche*. Local lobster also features strongly on many menus, though visitors should be aware that numbers have been declining locally, despite the strict controls placed on lobster fishing.

### DRINKS

Mexican beer *(cerveza)* is excellent and is a good thirst-quencher on hot sunny days. Beers are either light *(clara)* or dark *(negra)* and are usually drunk straight from the bottle with a slice of lime in the top. Popular brands include Sol, Corona and Montejo (all light) and Leon (dark). Imported wines are available in the better restaurants, but Mexican wine is also worth trying. For those who want something a bit stronger, tequila is a fiery spirit produced from the fermented juice of the agave plant. It is traditionally drunk neat accompanied by a pinch of salt and a twist of lime, or sipped slowly in a margarita, a cocktail of tequila, triple sec, lime juice and crushed ice, served in a salt-rimmed glass. Mezcal is a variation of tequila, distinctive for the pickled agave worm at the bottom of the bottle, added as a sign of quality – only in good quality Mezcal does the worm stay intact.

## Restaurant Selection

The following are recommendations for the main centers, listed alphabetically, according to the following categories: $$$ (expensive); $$ (moderate); $ (inexpensive).

### Campeche

**Marganzo**, Calle 8 No 262, tel: (981) 811-3898. Typical regional food, served by waitresses dressed in regional costumes. $$.

**La Pigua**, Malecón Miguel Alemán No 197-A, tel: (981) 811-3365. Excellent seafood and regional cuisine served in a glass conservatory. $$.

### Cancún Hotel Zone

**Blue Bayou**, Hyatt Cancún Caribe Hotel, Blvd. Kukulcán km 12.5, tel: (998) 848-7800. Cajun, Creole and international cuisine served in a tropical garden. $$–$$$.

**Captain's Cove**, Royal Plaza & Marina, Blvd. Kukulcán km 16.5, tel: (998) 885-0016. Fresh seafood dishes in palapa-style setting, with beautiful view of the lagoon. $$–$$$.

**Carlos'n Charlie's**, Blvd. Kukulcán km 5.5, tel: (998) 849-4057. Part of a restaurant chain, combining international and Mexican cuisine. Musical and other entertainment. $–$$.

**Casa Rolandi**, Plaza Caracol, Blvd. Kukulcán km 8.5, tel: (998) 883-2557. Fine Northern Italian cuisine; a Cancún institution. $$$.

**Jonny Rockets**, La Isla Shopping Village, Blvd. Kukulcán km 12.5. American-style diner with great burgers. $.

**Mayan Restaurant Pacal**, La Mansion-Costa Blanca Shopping Center, Blvd. Kukulcán km 8.5, tel: (998) 883-2184. Caribbean cuisine, fresh seafood and Yucatecan specialties. $$$.

**Plantation House**, Blvd. Kukulcán km 10.5, tel: (998) 883-1455. Caribbean seafood specialties in a sophisticated setting overlooking the Nichupté lagoon. **$$$**.

**Ruth's Chris Steak House**, Kukulcán Plaza, Blvd. Kukulcán km 13, tel: (998) 885-3301. Internationally acclaimed for its prime steak; also try the blackened tuna. **$$$**.

**Señor Frog's**, Blvd. Kukulcán km 9.5, tel: (998) 883-1092. Enjoy the party atmosphere in this popular restaurant. Part of a chain, also at La Isla. **$–$$**.

### Cancún Downtown

**Carlos O'Brian's**, Av. Tulum 29, tel: (998) 884-1659. Casual dining in a lively atmosphere. **$$**.

**La Habichuela**, Margaritas 25, tel: (998) 884-3158. Award-winning restaurant serving seafood with a Caribbean touch in a beautiful garden. **$$$**.

**La Placita**, Av. Yaxchilan 12, tel: (998) 884-6315. Seafood and steaks and the best tacos in Cancún. **$–$$**.

**Rolandi's**, Av. Cobá 12, tel: (998) 884-4047. Known to offer the best pizza in town. **$–$$**.

### Cozumel

**Acuario**, Av Rafael E Melgar, corner Calle 11 south. Popular restaurant with oceanfront seafood dining. **$$**.

**Azul Cobalto**, Av. Juarez 181, tel: (987) 872-3318. International cuisine and great pizza. **$–$$**.

**El Capi Navegante**, Av. 10 Sur No 312, tel: (987) 872-1730. One of the local seafood favorites. **$$**.

**Casa Denis**, Calle 1 Sur No 132, tel: (987) 872-0067. Long-established restaurant serving authentic Yucatecan food, tacos and seafood. **$**.

**Guido's** (formerly Pizza Rolandi), Av Rafael E Melgar, tel: (987) 872-0946. Great Italian food; excellent pizza. **$$**.

**Las Palmeras**, Av. Melgar/Juarez, tel: (987) 872-0532. A long time favorite near the ferry pier that's always busy. Well-presented international food. **$$**.

**Rock N Java Cafe**, Av Rafael E Melgar No 602, tel: (987) 872-4405. Wonderful breakfast, great sandwiches, breads, croissants and cakes. **$**.

### Isla Mujeres

**Restaurant-Bar Amigos**, Av Miguel Hidalgo No 19, tel: (998) 877-0624. Good Mexican/international cuisine at reasonable prices. **$–$$**.

**La Cazuela**, Hotel Roca Mar, Calle Nicolas Bravo and Zona Maritima, tel: (998) 877-0101. A variety of delicious and innovative combinations. **$$**.

**La Lorena**, Avenida Guerrero. Fine restaurant in a renovated clapboard house serving pasta, salads and seafood. **$$–$$$**.

*Watering hole at Playa del Carmen*

> **Saturday night fever**
> On Saturday nights, Mérida's Calle 60 is closed to traffic and the restaurants spill out onto the street. Whether you want fine dining or simple tacos, it's all here, to the accompaniment of much music and merriment.

**Rolandi's**, Av. Hidalgo 110, tel: (998) 877-0430. One of a popular local chain serving pizzas and other dishes. **$$**.

**Zazil-Ha**, Zazil-Ha 118, tel: (998) 877-0279. Eat either inside or outside at this pleasant restaurant in the Hotel Na Balam, serving Mexican, traditional Maya and seafood dishes. **$$**.

### Izamal
**Tumben-Lol**, Calle 22 No 302 between 31 and 33, tel: (988) 954-0231. Regional dishes in an airy palapa. **$**.

**Kinich Kakmó**, Calle 27 No 299 between 28 and 30, tel: (988) 954-0489. Yucatecan cuisine in a typical colonial mansion. **$$**.

### Mérida
**Café Alameda**, Calle 58 No 474, between 55 and 57, tel: (999) 928-3635. Best Lebanese cuisine in Mérida. **$**.

**Los Almendros**, Calle 50 No 493 between 57 and 59, tel: (999) 923-8135. Founded in Ticul, this restaurant is famous for its Yucatecan cuisine. **$$**.

**Amaro**, Calle 59 between 60 and 62, tel: (999) 928-2451. Good local and international cuisine served in a pleasant open courtyard. **$–$$**.

**La Bella Epoca**, Calle 60 No 495 between 57 and 59, tel: (999) 928-1928. Good regional and international cuisine in the pleasant atmosphere of the Hotel del Parque. **$$**.

**Casa de Piedra**, in Hacienda Xcanatun, km12 Mérida-Progreso Road, tel: (999) 941-0213. Top class international, Caribbean and Yucatecan cuisine in a beautiful hacienda. **$$$**.

**Hosteria L'Fondiu**, Calle 52 No 469 between 53 and 51, tel: (999) 924-9149. Inexpensive Mexican and regional dishes. Open 8am–2pm. **$**.

**Muelle 8**, Calle 21 No 141, tel: (999) 944-5343. One of Mérida's best seafood restaurants. **$$**.

### Playa del Carmen
**Blue Parrott**, Calle 12 on the beachfront, tel: (984) 873-0083. Top quality international cuisine. **$$$**.

**Coffee Press**, 5th Avenue, corner of Calle 2. Excellent breakfasts. **$**.

**Las Mañanitas**, 5th Avenue between Calles 4 and 6, tel: (984) 873-0114. Excellent Mexican and international cuisine served with Italian flair. **$$**.

**100% Natural**, 5th Avenue between 10 and 12, tel: (984) 873-2242. Franchise of the popular natural food chain in a pleasant open courtyard. **$**.

**Palapa Hemingway**, 5th Avenue between 12 and 14, tel: (984) 803-0004. Specializes in Cuban cuisine. **$$**.

**La Parrilla**, 5th Avenue, corner of Calle 8, tel: (984) 873-0687. Famous restaurant specializing in grilled seafood and meats. Mariachi musicians every night. **$$–$$$**.

**Yax Che**, Calle 8 between 5th and 10th Avenues, tel: (984) 873-2502. Refined Maya cuisine. **$$–$$$**.

### Tulum
**Don Cafeto**, Av. Tulum No 64, tel: (984) 871-2272. Good Mexican and international fare on Highway 307 through town; excellent desserts. **$–$$**.

### Valladolid
**El Caribe**, Calle 49 No 251 between 52 and 54, tel: (985) 856-1349. Meats and seafood; Yucatecan fare. **$$**.

**Mesón de Marqués**, Calle 39 No 203 between 40 and 42, tel: (985) 856-2073. Delightful courtyard restaurant in the hotel of the same name, serving Yucatecan specialties. **$–$$**.

# NIGHTLIFE

Nightlife in Cancún takes on a variety of forms, from shows of folkloric music and dance to state of-the-art dance clubs. Isla Mujeres and Cozumel are more low key, but Playa del Carmen has a burgeoning nightlife scene.

## TRADITIONAL ENTERTAINMENT

The **Teatro de Cancún** (Blvd. Kukulcán Km 4, www.elembarcadero.com) offers its shows *Voces y Danzas de México* and *Tradición del Caribe* every night from Mon–Fri at 7pm and 9pm. Incidentally, followers of traditional Mexican music and dance can also see it spectacularly performed at Xcaret as part of the evening show *(see page 38)*.

An even more varied palette of music and dance can be found in Mérida, where there are free performances at different locations in the city center every night of the week, ranging from traditional music and dance, to big band music to *ballet folklórico (see page 71)*.

## HOT SPOTS

Nightclubs of Cancún include the giant **Coco Bongo** (Plaza Forum, Blvd.Kukulcán Km 9.5. www.cocobongo.com.mx), famous for its non-stop show that includes everything from bubbles and foam to flying acrobats, with all the latest sound, light and special effects. Nearby **DadyO**, with its tiered seats, is another popular venue, as is **La Boom** (blvd Kukulcán Km 3.5, www.laboom.com.mx), which features a multi-level dance floor.

There are some good bars with live music such as **Pat O'Brien's** (Plaza Flamingo, Blvd. Kukulcán Km 11.5), a New Orleans themed bar with great piano music; and **Azúcar** (Punta Cancún, next to Camino Real Hotel), where you can dance to the rhythm of tropical live bands. Jazz & blues fans can head downtown to **Jazz Club Roots** (Calle Tulipanes 26, closed Sun), which also serves great food.

In Playa del Carmen, most of the nightlife is concentrated along **5th Avenue**. There are quiet bars, rowdy bars, bars on the beach, sports bars and bars with live music. Most of them close at 2am; night clubs and dance clubs are open a little longer. Sometimes, especially around full moon, all-night raves are arranged on the beach, quite often at **Coco Beach**.

*Traditional music performed at Xcaret*

# SHOPPING

## WHAT TO BUY

There is a huge variety of handicrafts on sale in the plazas of Cancún's hotel zone and the downtown markets. Much is locally produced and includes woven blankets, replica Maya artefacts, traditional clothing (embroidered dresses – *huipile* – for women and traditional, loose-fitting shirts – *guayabera* – for men. In addition, there are colorful ceramics, brightly painted masks, and models of clay, wood or papier mâché.

Mexico is still one of the world's largest producers of silver, and whether you're in Cancún, Playa del Carmen, Isla Mujeres or Cozumel, you'll see shops with an incredible choice of silver jewelry, ornaments, tea sets, goblets and trophies at very competitive prices (make sure that your purchase bears a stamp of the word Mexico and the number 925, this being the standard quality of silver found here). In addition to silver, Cozumel in particular is well-known for its competitively-priced gemstones which are sold along Avenida Rafael Melgar *(see page 46).*

*Hammocks, hats and rugs
for sale on Isla Mujeres*

You may feel tempted to buy a Yucatecan hammock. There is a bewildering range of quality, colors and sizes; try to go for a finely-woven hammock with thin threads; the roughly woven ones with big holes might be cheaper but they're nowhere near as comfortable.

## WHERE TO BUY

To visit the genuine, colorful atmosphere of a Mexican market, visit the **Hi Kuic** craft market in Cancún *(see page 27)*, or better still the **Mercado Municipal** in Mérida (corner of calle 56 and 67), where a number of shops under one roof sell a huge variety of crafts. Also in Mérida is the government run **Casa de las Artesanias** *(see page 70)*, together with numerous other handicraft shops dotted around Plaza Grande. In Valladolid there is a good crafts shop, **Artesanias Ek Balam** (corner Calles 39 and 40).

Some towns have their own specialties, such as Ticul with its ceramics *(see page 80)*. For exquisite reproductions of Maya vases, masks and other artefacts, call in at **Los Ceibos** in Muna (Calle 13, in front of the Chun Yaax Che restaurant, *see page 80)*.

# ACTIVE PURSUITS

**Protect the reefs!**
Novice snorkelers will usually be taken to sections of reef where the water is quite shallow. Avoid the temptation of standing up or touching the coral with any part of your body; it is easy to destroy in seconds something that has taken years for nature to create. Most good dive centers provide buoyancy aids for novices.

## SNORKELING

You don't have to be experienced to enjoy the wonders of the Mesoamerican reef system *(see pages 12–13)*. Simply book an excursion on a boat operated by a recognized dive center (see opposite for a selection). You will usually be given a guided snorkel tour, the guide pointing out the many different kinds of fish and coral. Centers hire out equipment, but you may prefer to bring your own.

A popular destination on Isla Mujeres is the Lighthouse Reef at the northwest tip of the island. Cancún offers the reef off Punta Nizuc, amongst others, and there are several shallow sections of reef good for snorkeling just north of Playa del Carmen.

There is also good snorkeling from the shore in certain places, notably at Garrafón/Punta Sur on Isla Mujeres; at Akumal on the Riviera; and along the west coast of Cozumel (Chankabaab Beach Park, Playa San Francisco and Playa Palancar). The inlets of Xcaret, Xel-Ha and Tres Ríos are also excellent places to go snorkeling.

## DIVING

Cozumel is regarded as the jewel among the region's diving areas. Off the west coast there are 30km (20 miles) of reefs, at different depths and offering varying levels of difficulty. They include the famous Palancar, Colombia and Chankanaab reefs. There are also excellent dive sites off Isla Mujeres (Manchones and La Bandera reefs), Cancún and Playa del Carmen.

Remember to bring your dive certificate, as you will only be allowed to rent equipment and dive if you can prove your competence. But you can also learn to dive with one of the many dive centers, which are usually affiliated with PADI (Professional Association of Diving Instructors). Here are some recommendations:

**Diving Adventures**, Calle 5 Sur No 22, Cozumel, tel: (987) 872-3009, www.divingadventures.net

**AquaWorld**, tel: (998) 848-8326, www.aquaworld.com.mx An organization that offers a host of activities in addition to diving and snorkeling; also at Cozumel and Isla Mujeres.

**Scuba Cancún**, Blvd Kukulcán Km 5, Cancún, tel: (998) 849-7508, www.scubacancun.com.mx

**Sea Friends**, Av. Hidalgo s/n, Playa Norte, Isla Mujeres, tel: (998) 842-5348. Located on Playa Norte and run by champion free-diver Felipe Garrido.

**Phantom Divers**, Primera Avenida Norte/ Calle 14, Playa del Carmen, tel: (984) 879-3988; mobile: (984) 806-5829; www.phantomdivers.com

## EXPLORING THE CAVERNS

The freshwater cenotes and caverns of the peninsula offer another, fascinating dimension to diving and snorkeling. A number of dive companies offer excursions, or you can go direct to Hidden Worlds Cenotes *(see page 41)*, which runs diving and snorkeling tours into the world's largest system of underwater caverns, just north of Tulum. Even novice snorkelers can admire the cavernous, crystal-clear depths here; for divers an open water certificate is sufficient. **Hidden Worlds**, tel: (984) 877-8535, www.hiddenworlds.com.mx

## FISHING

The warm waters of the Caribbean are teeming with fish, including sailfish, tuna, and several species of marlin (most common between March and June). Large deep-sea fishing boats are based at AquaWorld *(see previous page)* and Xcaret, and at many other places along the coast. Operators practice catch and release, and special hooks ensure that the fish are not harmed. You can also go fly-fishing in the Nichupté Lagoon and the lagoons of the Sian Ka'an Biosphere Reserve *(see box)*, where catching four different types of fish (bonefish, permit, snook and tarpon) constitutes a so-called Grand Slam.

## SWIMMING WITH DOLPHINS

This is becoming increasingly popular, though it is very expensive. Dolphin Discovery (www.dolphindiscovery.com) operates centers on Isla Mujeres, Cozumel and at Puerto Aventuras; there are also facilities at Xcaret and Xel-Há (www.viadelphi.com), and at La Isla

*Snorkeling trip off Playa del Carmen*

### Sian Ka'an

It is possible to venture into the wilderness of the Sian Ka'an Biosphere Reserve *(see page 12)*, where you can do a variety of activities such as snorkeling and diving, sport fishing, kayaking and birdwatching. Tours are available locally at the village of Punta Allen at the end of the very bumpy Boca Paila Road south of Tulum *(see page 43)*. Contact Amigos de Sian Ka'an in Cancún (tel: 998 884-9583) for further details.

Shopping Village and Parque Nizuc, both in Cancún.

## BIRDWATCHING

The coastal lagoons, including those at the reserves of Celestún and Río Lagartos, provide rich habitats for birds. At Celestún contact the **Cultur** visitors' center for birdwatching tours; at Río Lagartos, which is less developed, it's best to go with recognized guides such as Diego Martínez and Ismael Navarro, who are based at the **Restaurant Isla Contoy** (tel: 986 862-0000, www.ismaelnavarro.gobot.com), or the Marfíl brothers who operate **Flamingo Tours** on the waterfront (flamingos-tours-rio@hotmail.com). As well as birdwatching tours, you can go night-time crocodile spotting at Río Lagartos.

# PRACTICAL INFORMATION

## Getting There

### BY AIR

From North America there are many daily connections to hubs or directly to Cancún. Try the following airlines: US Airways (www.usairways.com); United Airlines (www.ual.com); American Airlines (www.aa.com); Continental (www.flycontinental.com); Aeromexico (www.aeromexico.com); Mexicana (www.mexicana.com). These airlines may offer packages in addition to flights.

The choice of direct, non-stop flights from the UK is limited to package tour operators such as Airtours and First Choice. However, there are other options, including with Martinair (www.martinair.com) from Amsterdam (booked from London through KLM – www.klm.com) and Iberia (www.iberia.es) from London via Madrid to Cancún. Alternatively, Cancún can be reached via Miami or Mexico City and an onward connecting flight. Travelers heading for Cozumel, Playa del Carmen or Mérida transfer to local carriers like Aerocaribe (www.aerocaribe.com) at Cancún. It is usually cheaper to book the onward internal flight together with your main flight.

Cancún International Airport is situated 20km (12 miles) south of the city. Your hotel may have a courtesy bus to pick you up at the airport; otherwise you can take a mini-bus *(colectivo)* either to the Hotel Zone or downtown. They run about every 30 minutes, and you can buy your tickets at the kiosk in the arrivals area; the price is around US$10. The alternative here is to take a taxi, but fares from the airport tend to be expensive.

**Departure tax**: Be aware that a departure tax is levied on many flights out of Cancún. This is quite high, and payable in cash (dollars or pesos).

### BY SHIP

Cozumel and the Riviera Maya are becoming increasingly important cruise destinations for Caribbean cruise ships operating out of Miami, Puerto Rico and elsewhere. Carnival and Celebrity are the main cruise lines involved, and they berth either at Cozumel or at the port at Calica just to the south of Playa del Carmen.

## Getting Around

### BY BUS

As with the rest of Mexico, the Yucatán has very well organized bus transport. The Cancún–Tulum corridor to Playa del Carmen and Tulum along Highway 307 is served mainly by the **Riviera** bus company, which is based at the main bus terminal in Cancún (corner Avenida Tulum/Avenida Uxmal), and usually stops at Puerto Morelos, Xcaret, and Xel-Há. The second class **Oriente** company serves the route between Cancún and Mérida, while **ADO**, with its luxury first-class GL buses, serves all the major towns and cities in the region.

Note that while there is only one major bus station in Cancún, there are several in Mérida. These include the Terminal CAME at Calles 70 and 71 for first-class buses; the Terminal de Autobuses at Calle 69 between 68 and 70 for second-class buses, and the Terminal de Autobuses del Oriente, Oriente's main terminal at Calle 50 between 65 and 67. Further bus stations in Mérida serve the northeast (e.g. Río Lagartos), Progreso and Celestún.

With their soft seats and air conditioning, second-class buses should be comfortable enough for most travelers. Prices are relatively cheap (Cancún–Playa del Carmen around 35 pesos).

## FERRIES

The main ferry departure point for Isla Mujeres is at Puerto Juarez just to the north of downtown Cancún. Express ferries run once every half hour *(see page 28)*. The main jumping off point for Cozumel is Playa del Carmen, from where a passenger ferry operates every half hour. There is a car ferry that operates out of Puerto Morelos, but few visitors use this service as cars can easily be hired on Cozumel.

## BY CAR

Car rental in Mexico is expensive by international standards, but it is a good option if you intend to travel around the interior of the Yucatán, enabling you to explore the lands of the Maya in your own time. Car hire companies represented in the main tourist areas include Avis, Hertz, Budget, Dollar, Executive, National and Localiza. It pays to shop around. Watch out for terms of insurance – excess charges on fully comprehensive cover, for instance. To hire a car you will need to hold a current valid driver's licence and be over 21; national driver's licences are accepted. Note that car hire is considerably cheaper in the low season.

**Road conditions**: The roads in the Yucatán are generally good, though the seasonal rains can cause potholing. The main toll road *(carretera de cuota)* in the Yucatán runs parallel to Highway 180 between Cancún and Mérida. It's a fast way of crossing the northern Yucatán, but also expensive – and if you take it you'll miss out on some interesting places along the way.

**Rules of the road**: The speed limit on open country roads is 80km/h (50mph); on motorways 110km/h (70mph); towns and villages 40km/h (25mph); Cancún Hotel Zone (Blvd. Kukulcán) 60km/h (40mph). It is best to avoid driving at night as there are too many unlit obstacles such as live-stock and cyclists. In case of accident or breakdown, the Green Angels highway patrol *(Angeles Verdes)* will come to your rescue, tel: (800) 903-0092 (toll-free).

**Fuel**: The only gas stations are Pemex, which are state controlled. Cash payments only.

**Speed bumps**
If you're traveling by car, beware of the *topes* (speed bumps), which straddle the roads on the way into towns and villages. Though they are clearly signed, they often come in series, so just when you think you've crossed the last one, another one may be there lurking and ready to cause considerable damage to your suspension if you're driving too fast.

# Facts for the Visitor

## TRAVEL DOCUMENTS

American and Canadian visitors can enter Mexico with their passport or birth certificate accompanied by a photo ID. Visitors from other countries normally only require a passport valid for at least six months. On arrival you will be issued with a Mexican Tourist Permit (usually valid for 30 days), which must be kept and submitted to the authorities on departure.

## TOURIST INFORMATION

The Mexican Secretariat of Tourism (SECTUR) operates across the US plus other select countries around the world. These offices offer a wide range of services to assist visitors.

**In the US**: 21 East 63rd Street, 3rd Floor, New York, NY 10021, tel: (212) 821-0314, fax: (212) 821-0367. 1200 N.W. 78th Avenue, Suite 203, Miami, FL. 33126, tel: (305) 718-4091, fax: (305) 718-4098. 1010 Fomdren St, Houston, TX 77096, tel: (713) 772-2581, fax: (713) 772-6058. 300

N. Michigan, 4th Floor, Chicago, IL 60601, tel: (312) 606-9252, fax: (312) 606-9012. 2401 W. 6th St., 5th Floor Los Angeles, CA 90057, tel: (213) 351-2075, fax: (213) 351-2074. The toll free number for the US is 1-800-44-MEXICO.

**In the UK**: Wakefield House, 41 Trinity Street, London EC3N 4JD, tel: (020) 7488-9392, fax: (020) 7265-0704.

**In Mexico**: there are also state tourist offices for Campeche, Quintana Roo and Yucatán, plus the more useful local tourist offices in Cancún (22 Avenida Tulum, tel: 998 884-8073) and Mérida (Calle 60 below the Péon Contreras Theatre and in the Governor's Palace). In addition, there are a wide variety of information magazines and brochures available, including the informative *Yucatán Today* for Mérida, and *Cancún Tips* available all over Cancún. Playa del Carmen, Tulum, Akumal and other resorts also have their own information magazines.

## LANGUAGE

Spanish is the official language, but English is widely spoken in the resort areas. The rural population is bilingual, speaking Maya (of which there are numerous dialects) and Spanish.

## ELECTRICITY

The electricity standard is 110 volt AC, the same as in the US and Canada. Although three-prong outlets are available in some places, it is always a good idea to bring an adaptor.

## TIME ZONE

The Yucatán Peninsula is on Central Standard Time, 6 hours behind GMT. Daylight saving time is from May to September.

## CURRENCY AND EXCHANGE

The Mexican unit of currency is the peso, which is abbreviated to $, which can make prices confusing, though US-dollar prices are usually quoted with the abbreviation USD. Notes come in 20, 50, 100, 200 and 500 denominations; coins in denominations of 1, 2, 5, 10 and 20 pesos and 5,10, 20 and 50 centavos.

Exchange offices *(casas de cambio)* will exchange euros and pounds as well as dollars, but banks usually have a preference for dollars – if you're taking travelers' cheques it's best to have them in dollars. Many of the major attractions, such as Xcaret, accept payment in dollars, so it's useful to have some cash dollars with you as well. The easiest (and cheapest) way of obtaining local currency is by using an ATM machine with your debit/credit card. Any major bank such as Banamex, found in most towns, will have an ATM inside; machines are also strategically located in Cancún's shopping plazas. Credit cards are widely accepted for payment in shops, restaurants and at the attractions in the main resorts. Outside these areas, always ask whether they are accepted.

## TIPPING

Because the wages are low in Mexico, service personnel rely on money earned in tips. 10–15 percent is standard in restaurants; hotel maids, porters, car park and gas station attendants should also be tipped.

### Addresses

Most Yucatecan towns are laid out on a grid pattern, with even-numbered streets running in one direction and odd numbers in another. Addresses are pinpointed by stating the street plus the two cross streets between which the actual house number can be found. Thus, for example, the address of the Casa de las Artesanías in Mérida is Calle 63 # 503 x 64 y 66 (street 63 number 503 between streets 64 and 66).

## OPENING TIMES

Banks in Cancún and other main centers are open weekdays from 9am to 5pm, and some are open on Saturday from 10am to 2pm. Banks in smaller towns usually close at 1pm.

Stores in tourist areas are generally open until 8 or 9pm, even longer in Cancún and Playa del Carmen. Shops not in the main tourist areas will close for siesta between 2pm and 4pm.

Archeological sites are generally open daily 8am–5pm. Note that there is no entrance fee on Sundays, but at Chichén Itzá and Uxmal there is no Sound & Light Show either.

## PUBLIC HOLIDAYS

Banks, government offices, schools and many stores close on the following dates: January 1 (New Year's Day); February 5 (Constitution Day); March 21 (Birthday of Benito Juárez); Easter; May 1 (Labor Day); September 1 (Informe Presidencial – first day of Congress); September 16 (Independence Day); October 12 (Día de la Raza – Columbus Day); November 2 (Day of the Dead); November 20 (Revolution Day); December 25 (Christmas Day).

## TELEPHONE

The country code for Mexico is 52, preceded by 011 if calling from the US or Canada; 00 if calling from the UK. Recent changes to codes in Mexico mean that all area codes are now 3-digit, followed by a 7-digit number. If dialing within the area, there is no need to dial the code. The easiest way of calling locally or internationally is to use a Telmex phonecard, available for $30, $50 and $100 at most groceries and newsagents and usable at the ubiquitous Ladatel payphones.

## SECURITY AND CRIME

The Yucatán is a very safe place, and you have a greater chance of being robbed by other tourists than by locals. In case of difficulty, Mérida has its own Tourist Police who patrol the central area (tel: 925-2555, ext 260). Other police numbers are: Cancún, 884-2342; Isla Mujeres, 877-0458; Playa del Carmen 873-0291; Cozumel, tel: 872-0409.

**Consulates in Cancún**: UK, tel: 881-0100, ext 65898; US, tel: 883-0272.

## MEDICAL

Always take out adequate insurance to cover emergency health problems. There are no specific innoculation requirements, though if you're going to spend a lot of time in the jungle you might consider a course of anti-malaria pills. Do not drink the local tap water *(see below)*, always carry insect repellent and/or mosquito coils if you're traveling around, and ensure you have adequate protection from the bright sun.

**Pharmacies and hospitals**: There are plenty of pharmacies *(farmacia)* for over-the-counter drugs; if you need to see a doctor, inform the staff at your hotel and they will call for assistance. There are good hospitals in Cancún (Hospital Americano, tel: 884-6133) and in Mérida (Centro Médico de la Americas, tel: 927-3199).

**Water and ice**
Times have moved on and the water you are served at a restaurant or the ice that goes in your juice or *licuado* is all *agua purificada* (purified water), and thus perfectly safe. Salads are prepared using *agua purificada*, so they, too, are safe. This applies not just to Cancún, but all towns with a restaurant trade. There may be the odd exception that proves the rule, and you shouldn't push your luck with roadside juice sellers, for example, but the days of Montezuma's revenge are almost gone.

# ACCOMMODATION

From the giant international hotels of Cancún to simple guesthouses and beach cabañas, the region offers a huge choice of accommodation. Prices are higher during the high season *(see page 8)*, when advanced booking is recommended; during the low season it pays to look around; there are good deals to be had, particularly at the coastal resorts.

## Hotel Selection

The following are recommendations for the main centers. They are listed alphabetically, according to the following price categories: $$$$ (very expensive); $$$ (expensive); $$ (moderate); $ (inexpensive).

### Campeche

**Hotel America**, Calle 10 No 252, tel: (981) 816-4588, fax: 811-0556. Pleasant hotel in 2-story colonial mansion in downtown Campeche. $–$$.

**Hotel Del Mar Ramada**, Av. Ruiz Cortines 51, tel: (981) 816-2233. Large, modern hotel near the seafront. $$–$$$.

### Cancún

**Blue Lagoon**, Blvd. Kukulcán km. 7.8, tel: (998) 883-1215. Comfortable accommodation in the only modestly-priced hotel in the middle of the hotel zone; individual balconies. $$.

**Fiesta Americana Condesa Cancún**, Blvd. Kukucán, km 16.5, tel: (998) 881-4200, fax: 885-2014, www.fiestaamericana.com A beautiful hotel with a warm, Mediterranean-Mexican style atmosphere and world-class quality and service. $$$–$$$$.

**Hilton Beach Cancún**, Blvd. Kulkucán, km 17, tel: (998) 881-8000, fax: 881-8093, www.hiltoncancun.com Enormous, pyramid-style luxury hotel with seven swimming pools, its very own golf course and within close proximity to the El Rey ruins. $$$$.

**Meliá Cancún Convention Center & Spa Resort**, Blvd. Kulkucán, km 16.5, tel: (998) 881-1100, fax: 881-1720, www.solmelia.es Spectacular hotel with three pyramids; rooms with either ocean or lagoon views. $$$–$$$$.

**Park Royal Pirámides Cancún**, Blvd. Kukulcán km 12.5, tel: (998) 885-1333, fax: 8850113, www.piramidescancun.com.mx Pyramid-style construction just steps away from important shopping centers, nightclubs and restaurants. $$$.

**Plaza Cancún**, Blvd. Kukulcán km 11.5, tel: (998) 881-5500, fax: 881-5695. Attractive Mediterranean-style hotel with three restaurants and two swimming pools, plus a villa section. $$$.

**El Pueblito Beach Cancún**, Blvd. Kulkucán, km 17.5, tel: (998) 885-0422, fax: 885-0731. Thoughtfully designed Mexican-style hotel set along one of Cancún's best beaches. Five swimming pools. $$$.

**Villas Tacul**, Blvd. Kulkucán, km 5.5, tel: (998) 883-0000, fax: 849-7070, www.villastacul.com.mx Intimate, secluded oasis of one-to-five bedroom villas set in lush and tranquil gardens. $$$.

### Cancún Downtown

**Hotel Colonial**, Tulipanes 22, tel: (998) 884-1535. Basic but clean hotel in the Tulipanes pedestrian zone with plenty of restaurants nearby. $–$$.

**Hotel Cotty**, Av. Uxmal No 44, tel: (998) 884-0550. Long established, family-run hotel with reasonable rates and facilities, including cable TV, just 100m from the bus station. $–$$.

**Holiday Inn**, Av. Nader 1 S.M. 2, tel: (998) 887-4455, fax: 884-7954. Holiday Inn comforts in a building inspired by hacienda architecture. $$$.

**Mexico Hostels**, Corner Av. Uxmal/Palmera, tel: (998) 887-0191. Cheap hostel with good facilities including kitchen and TV, just four blocks from the bus station. $.

**El Patio**, Av. Bonampak No 51 & Calle Cereza, tel: (998) 884-3500, fax: 884-3540. Impeccable small hotel with a colonial atmosphere; only 18 rooms surrounding a lush patio. $$.

### Celestún

**Eco Paraiso**, on the old road to Sisal km 10, tel: (988 )916-2100, fax: 916-2060, www.ecoparaiso.com Beautifully designed bungalows near the beach, surrounded by a coconut grove and next to the national park. $$$.

### Chichén Itzá

**Hacienda Chichén**, Zona Arqueológica, tel (Mérida): (999) 924-2150; fax: 924-5011. Delightful 16th-century hacienda, once home to archeologist Edward Thompson; accommodation in bungalows with private terraces. $$$.

**Mayaland**, Chichén Itzá, Zona Arqueológica, tel: (985) 851-0128, fax: 851-0129. Designed in traditional Maya style, this 5-star hotel is located in landscaped grounds adjacent to the site, with its own entrance. $$$.

*The Hilton Beach Cancún*

**Posada Chac-Mool**, Highway 180, Pisté. Cheap and clean accommodation 2 km (1 mile) from the site. $.

### Cozumel

**Amigo's B&B Cozumel**, Calle 7 Sur No 571-A, tel: (987) 872-3868, fax: 872-3528. Located on a quiet street five blocks from the ocean; rooms feature a kitchenette and private bath. $–$$.

**Fiesta Americana Cozumel Dive Resort**, Carr. Chankanaab km 7.5, tel: (987) 872-2622, fax: 872-2666, fiestaamericana.com Beachfront resort facing the world-famous Palancar Reef and located only minutes from restaurants, shopping and nightlife. $$$.

**Flamingo Hotel**, Calle 6 Norte No 81, tel: (987) 872-1264. Centrally-located hotel in the colonial style, with rooftop terrace overlooking the Caribbean. $$.

**Hacienda San Miguel**, Calle 10 Norte No 500, between 5th Avenue and the Rafael Melgar, tel: (987) 872-1986, fax: 872-7043. A hidden treasure with lush gardens and rooms ranging from small studios to large suites. $$–$$$.

**Melia Mayan Paradisus**, Carr. Costera Norte km 5.8, tel: (987) 872-0411, fax: 872-1599, www.solmelia.es All-inclusive beach resort 10 minutes north of San Miguel; restaurants, watersports and nightly entertainment. $$$–$$$$.

**Playa Azul**, Carr. San Juan km 4,

Zona Hotelera Norte, tel: (987) 872-0033, fax: 872-0110, www.playa-azul.com Exclusive, intimate hotel located on the beautiful beach of San Juan; includes La Terraza restaurant. $$$–$$$$.

## Isla Mujeres

**Hotel Marcianito**, Calle Abasolo No 10, tel: (998) 877-0111. Pleasant, family-owned hotel in downtown Isla Mujeres. Shared balconies. $–$$.

**Na-Balam**, Calle Zazil-Há No. 118, tel: (998) 877-0279, fax: 877-0446, www.nabalam.com Located at the eastern end of Playa Norte, with 12 pool-side and 18 beachfront rooms. $$$.

**Hotel Playa la Media Luna**, Punta Norte, tel: (998) 877-0759, fax: 877-1124, www.playamedialuna.com Located on Half Moon Beach in the northeast of the island, a two-minute walk from Playa Norte. 18 rooms, each with balcony; pool. $$$.

**Condominios Playa Norte**, Chez Magaly, Nautibeach, Av. Rueda Medina, tel: (998) 877-0259, fax: 877-0487. Attractive two-bedroom units right on Playa Norte. $$–$$$.

**Villa Rolandi**, Carretera Sac Bajo, tel: (998) 877-0500, fax: 877-0100, www.villarolandi.com Exclusive hotel on the west coast of the island, with its own Casa Rolandi restaurant. $$$.

**Hotel Secreto**, Punta Norte, tel: (998) 877-1039, fax: 877-1048, www.hotelsecreto.com Small, elegant, luxury hotel in the northeast of the island with nine air-conditioned suites and pool. Non-smoking. $$$.

**Vistalmar**, Av Rueda Medina S/N, tel: (998) 877-0209, fax: 877-0096. Long-established hotel near the ferry dock. Ideal for those on a tight budget. $.

## Izamal

**Green River Hotel**, Av. Zamna 342, tel: (988) 954-0337. Comfortable rooms in attractive setting with air-conditioning, fridge and cable TV.

### Haciendas

Many of the region's haciendas, located in the 'henequen belt' around Mérida, have been restored and converted into fine hotels, providing relaxing stays in the heart of the Yucatán countryside. Some are run by, and can usually only be booked through, large organizations (Haciendas Temozón, San José, Uayamón and Santa Rosa – contact Grupo Plan in Mexico City, tel: (555) 257-0097, fax: (555) 257-0151; e-mail: info@grupoplan.com); others are locally-run properties, like Hacienda Katanchel or Hacienda Xcanatun *(see listings)*.

## Mérida

**Casa del Balam**, Calle 60, corner Calle 57, tel: (999) 924-2150. First-class hotel in the heart of Mérida with plenty of colonial antiques; beautiful patio gardens and pool. $$$.

**Luz en Yucatán**, Calle 55 No 499 between 58 and 60, tel: (999) 924-0035, www.luzenyucatan.com Single-story town-house in the heart of Mérida with tastefully furnished apartments and enticing pool. Yoga and other health & fitness activities available; cable TV. $–$$.

**Medio Mundo**, Calle 55 No 533 between 64 and 55, tel/fax: (999) 924-5472, www.hotelmediomundo.com Beautifully renovated 19th-century mansion with cool courtyard, terrace and pool; gorgeous rooms, breakfast included. $$.

**Hotel Meridano**, Calle 54 No 478, between 55 and 57, tel: (999) 923-2614. Centrally located, simple but clean budget accommodation. $.

**La Misión Fray Diego**, Calle 61 between 64 and 66, tel: (999) 924-11 11, www.lamisiondefraydiego.com Small, luxury hotel in a beautifully restored 17th-century residence with elegant rooms and wonderful grounds. $$$.

**Hotel Santa Ana**, Calle 45 No 503, between 60 and 62, tel: (999) 923-3331, www.hotelsantaana.com.mx Clean and pleasant, though not spectacular. $.

**Hacienda Katanchel**, km 26 Carr. Mérida–Cancún, tel: (999) 923-4020, fax: 923-4000, www.hacienda-katanchel.com Luxurious accommodation in pavilion suites amid 300 hectares (740 acres) of tropical forest. Grand salon, palatial dining room and billiard room. **$$$$**.

**Hacienda Xcanatun**, Km 12 Carretera Mérida–Progreso, tel: (999) 941-0213, www.xcanatun.com Refined elegance in a beautifully restored 18th-century hacienda; one of the great small hotels of the world. **$$$**.

### Playa del Carmen

**Copa Cabaña**, 5th Avenue No 209, between 10 and 12, tel & fax: (984) 873-0218, www.copacabanaplaya.net Good-value hotel with pleasant patio and hammocks outside every room. **$–$$**.

**Colibri**, 1A Avenida Norte between 10 and 12, tel: (984) 873-1833, www.hotel-colibri.com Hotel right on the beach, with spacious rooms and peaceful atmosphere; beach restaurant. **$$–$$$**.

**El Faro**, Calle 10 Norte, tel: (984) 873-0970, fax: (984) 873-0968, www.hotelelfaro.com. One of the best hotels in Playa, facing the beach with distinctive 'lighthouse' and 28 individually designed rooms. **$$$**.

**Hotel Lunata**, 5th Avenue between 6th and 8th Streets, tel: (984) 873-0884, fax: 873-1240, www.lunata.com Charming hacienda-style hotel in the heart of Playa del Carmen; a creative blend of the traditional and modern. **$$$**.

**Mosquito Blue**, 5th Avenue, between 12 and 14, tel: (984) 8731335. One of the first and best hotels in Playa, with stylish rooms and fabulous pool. No children under 16, however. **$$$**.

**Posada Las Iguanas**, Ave. Constituyentes and 5th Avenue, tel/fax: (984) 873-2170, www.posada-las-iguanas.com Reasonably-priced family-run establishment with lush gardens. **$–$$**.

**Quinto Sol**, 5th Avenue/Calle 28, tel: (984) 873-3292, www.hotelquintosol.com

Recent development at north end of 5th Avenue, a short walk from Playa Tucan; delightful tropical garden and roof-top palapa. **$$$**.

### Tulum

**Cabañas Ana Y José** , Carretera Boca Paila km 7, tel: (984) 887-5470. Cabañas on the beach, 7km (4 miles) south of Tulum. Laid-back atmosphere; swimming pool and restaurant. **$$**.

**Cabañas El Mirador**, Carretera Ruinas-Boca Paila km 0.7, no phone. Cheap cabañas with hammocks among the palm trees adjacent to the beach, half a mile south of the ruins. **$**.

**Maya Tulum**, Carretera Ruinas-Boca Paila km 7, tel: (984) 874-2772, www.mayatulum.com.mx Traditional Maya-style cabañas set in lush tropical gardens with beautiful views of the sea. **$$$**.

**Nohoch Tunich**, Carretera Boca Paila km 3.5, tel: (984) 871-2470. Hotel rooms and cabañas on small, secluded beach, with a restaurant. **$$**.

**Posada del Sol**, Carretera Boca Paila km 3.5, tel: (984) 806-6856. Beautiful little hotel opposite Nohoch Tunich. The four individually designed rooms utilize natural materials to best possible effect. **$$–$$$**.

### Uxmal

**Hotel Misión Uxmal**, Carr. Mérida-Campeche Km 78 Muna, Uxmal, tel: (997) 976-2022; fax: (997) 976-2023, www.hotelesmision.com Modern hotel with colonial-style features 1 km (½ mile) from the site. Great views. **$$$**.

### Valladolid

**Mesón de Marqués**, Calle 39 No 203 between 40 and 42, tel: (985) 856-2073. Old mansion on the main square with delightful courtyard; pool. **$$**.

**Hotel Zaci**, Calle 44 No 191, tel: (985) 856-2167. A well-kept neo-colonial hotel with comfortable rooms surrounding a lawn; courtyard with pool. **$**.

# The World of Insight Guides

## The world's largest collection of visual travel guides

Different people need different kinds of travel information.
Some want background facts. Others seek personal recommendations.
With a variety of different products — Insight Guides, Pocket Guides,
Compact Guides, Instant Guides, plus maps, phrasebooks and
dictionaries — we offer readers the perfect choice.
Insight Guides will turn your visit into an experience.

## ✹ INSIGHT GUIDES

# INDEX